ITALY ATLAS ROAD MAP 2025

Explore Italy City, With Accurate Atlas Road Map with Insider Tips to Navigate the City like Pro

MICHAEL WILLIAMS

Copyright © [2025] by [Michael Williams]

All rights reserved.

No part of this publication may be reproduced, stored in a retrieval system, or transmitted, in any form or by any means, electronic, mechanical, photocopying, recording, or otherwise, without the prior written permission of the publisher, except for brief quotations in critical reviews or article

TABLE OF CONTENT

INTRODUCTION 12
  Exploring Italy: A Land of Endless Wonders 12
  How to Use This Atlas Effectively 17
  Essential Road Trip Tips and Driving Etiquette in Italy
  20
  Overview of Italy's Road Infrastructure and Key
  Highways 23

CHAPTER ONE 26
  Understanding Italy's Road System 26
  Understanding Toll Roads in Italy 32
  Speed limits are strictly enforced using Tutor speed
  cameras. 33
  Road Signs, Fuel Stations, and EV Charging Points in
  Italy 38

CHAPTER TWO 46
  Planning Your Italian Road Trip 46
  Choosing the Right Vehicle: Car Rental, Camper Van, or
  Personal Car 50
  Parking in Italy: Rules, Apps, and Best Practices 🅿️□ .. 56
  Budgeting for Tolls, Fuel, and Accommodations 58
  Road Safety and Emergency Contact Numbers 62

CHAPTER THREE 66

Northern Italy Road Trips 66

Must-Visit Spots: Exploring Northern Italy's Alpine Gems 71

The Lakes Region Road Trip..75

The Milan to Venice Cultural Drive................................80

CHAPTER FOUR 94

The Tuscany and Chianti Wine Route: A Journey Through Italy's Heartland 94

🚗 The Best Route for Your Rome to Florence Road Trip 100

The Umbria and Marche Countryside Drive: A Journey Through Italy's Hidden Heart................................111

CHAPTER FIVE 132

The Amalfi Coast and Naples Drive: A Road Trip Through Italy's Most Breathtaking Coastline.............132

The Puglia and Matera Heritage Route: A Journey Through Italy's Timeless South...................................137

Exploring the Heart of Southern Italy: Bari, Alberobello, Matera & Gargano 142

Sicily's Grand Tour: A Journey Through Italy's Enchanting Island 147

CHAPTER SIX 160

Hidden Gems and Lesser-Known Routes...................160

🏔 Scenic Coastal Routes vs. Mountain Drives: Which One to Choose? 165

Best Villages and Countryside Retreats 166

🏰 Unique Road Trip Experiences 170

CHAPTER SEVEN 176

Practical Road Trip Tips and Resources 176

➔📱 Essential Apps for Navigation, Parking, and Fuel Stations 178

Packing Checklist, Road Etiquette, and Safety Tips for Travelers in Italy 181

IT Understanding Italian Road Etiquette and Customs 184

☐ Road Trip Safety: Theft Prevention, Avoiding Scams, and Traffic Stops 186

CHAPTER EIGHT 191

Interactive Maps and Itineraries for the Ultimate Italian Road Trip 192

🚗 Suggested Itineraries: 3-Day, 7-Day, and 14-Day Road Trips 194

Alternative Scenic Routes & Digital Resources for a Smooth Italian Road Trip 197

➔📱 QR Codes for Downloadable Maps & Real-Time Road Updates 200

CONCLUSION 202

Final Tips for an Unforgettable Italian Road Trip Experience 204

INTRODUCTION

Exploring Italy: A Land of Endless Wonders

Italy is an experience rather than merely a nation.From the snow-capped peaks of the Alps to the sun-drenched shores of the Amalfi Coast, every corner of this nation tells a story. Whether you're marveling at ancient Roman ruins, wandering through medieval villages, or indulging in world-famous cuisine, Italy captivates the heart and soul like no other place on Earth.

A road trip through Italy is the ultimate way to uncover its breathtaking landscapes, rich history, and vibrant culture. Unlike rigid tour schedules or rushed itineraries, driving gives you the freedom to move at your own pace, detour into charming small towns, and immerse yourself in authentic local life. Imagine sipping espresso in a sleepy Tuscan village, stumbling upon a centuries-old castle, or taking an impromptu swim in the crystal-clear waters of Sicily—these are the moments that make an Italian road trip unforgettable.

In this chapter, we'll explore the diverse geography, deep-rooted culture, and fascinating history of Italy, setting the stage for an adventure that promises to be as enlightening as it is exciting.

Italy's Diverse Geography: A Land of Contrasts

One of Italy's greatest appeals is its sheer geographic diversity. Unlike many European countries where landscapes tend to be uniform, Italy offers an extraordinary mix of natural wonders, making it a paradise for travelers with varied interests.

Northern Italy: Mountains, Lakes, and Alpine Charm

The northern region is dominated by the Alps and the Dolomites, home to some of the most breathtaking mountain landscapes in the world. Whether you're driving through Val Gardena, exploring the jagged peaks of Tre Cime di Lavaredo, or skiing in Cortina d'Ampezzo, the north offers dramatic scenery perfect for outdoor enthusiasts.

Just below the mountains, you'll find Italy's famous lakes, including Lake Como, Lake Garda, and Lake Maggiore. These sparkling waters are framed by charming lakeside towns, where cobbled streets, historic villas, and lush gardens create a postcard-perfect setting.

Central Italy: Rolling Hills, Vineyards, and Timeless Beauty

As you drive south, the rugged peaks give way to the rolling hills of Tuscany and Umbria. This is where you'll find Italy's famous wine country, home to sprawling vineyards and charming agriturismi (farm stays). Chianti, Montepulciano, and Montalcino are just a few of the world-renowned wine regions that beckon travelers to slow down and savor the moment.

Central Italy is also rich in history. Florence, the birthplace of the Renaissance, boasts world-class art and architecture, while medieval towns like Siena, San Gimignano, and Assisi transport visitors back in time with their well-preserved historical centers.

Southern Italy: Sun-Kissed Coasts and Ancient Mysteries

Southern Italy offers some of the most dramatic coastal drives in the world. The Amalfi Coast is a prime example, where roads carved into cliffs reveal breathtaking views of the Mediterranean Sea. Positano, Ravello, and Sorrento are must-visit stops along this scenic route.

Further south, Puglia is known for its whitewashed villages, like Alberobello, with its distinctive trulli houses, while Basilicata hides the stunning ancient cave city of Matera.

And then there's Sicily, Italy's largest island, where Greek temples, Baroque cities, and the imposing Mount Etna create an awe-inspiring backdrop.

Italy's Islands: Hidden Treasures in the Mediterranean

Beyond the mainland, Italy is home to over 450 islands, each with its own unique charm. Sardinia boasts some of Europe's most beautiful beaches, while smaller islands like Capri, Ischia, and the Aeolian Islands offer secluded escapes for those who seek paradise off the beaten path.

Whether you prefer mountains, lakes, rolling countryside, or coastal roads, Italy's geography ensures that every road trip is a new adventure.

Italy's Rich Culture: A Nation of Passion and Tradition

Italy is not just about stunning landscapes—it's also a country where tradition, art, and passion are woven into everyday life.

Food and Wine: A Culinary Journey

Each Italian region has its own distinct cuisine. In Naples, pizza is an art form. In Bologna, you'll find rich pasta dishes like tagliatelle al ragù (authentic Bolognese sauce). In Venice, seafood lovers can indulge in squid ink pasta.

Wine is equally important. Italy is one of the world's top wine producers, with over 350 official wine varieties. From the deep reds of Barolo in Piedmont to the crisp whites of Vermentino in Sardinia, each sip tells a story of the land and its people.

Festivals and Celebrations

Italy's calendar is packed with festivals that celebrate everything from religious traditions to food and music. The Venice Carnival, with its elaborate masks, is world-famous, while Palio di Siena, a medieval horse race, brings the Tuscan town to life twice a year.

For food lovers, the Truffle Festival in Alba and the Lemon Festival in Sorrento are must-visits.

Art, Music, and Timeless Creativity

Italy has gifted the world with some of the greatest artists, composers, and architects in history. From Michelangelo's Sistine Chapel to Leonardo da Vinci's Last Supper, the country is an open-air museum.

Music is just as important. Opera originated in Italy, and cities like Milan (La Scala) and Verona (Arena di Verona) host world-class performances year-round.

A Brief Look at Italy's Fascinating History

Italy's history spans over 3,000 years, making it one of the most historically significant countries in the world.

Ancient Rome: The Empire That Shaped the World

Rome, the Eternal City, was once the center of the world's greatest empire. The Colosseum, Roman Forum, and Pantheon still stand as reminders of its power.

The Renaissance: A Golden Age of Art and Science

The Renaissance (14th–17th centuries) was a period of groundbreaking achievements in art, science, and literature. Florence was at the heart of this movement, with artists like Leonardo da Vinci, Michelangelo, and Botticelli shaping the world's artistic legacy.

Modern Italy: A Unification of Regions

Italy as we know it today only became a unified country in 1861. Despite its unity, each region still retains its distinct identity, dialects, and traditions.

Why a Well-Planned Road Trip in Italy is Essential

With so much to see and experience, having a structured yet flexible road trip plan is key. Unlike other travel methods, a road trip allows you to:

✅ Explore at Your Own Pace – No rushing through crowded tourist spots. Take your time to truly enjoy each destination.

✅ Discover Hidden Gems – While major cities are incredible, the real magic often lies in lesser-known villages and scenic routes.

✅ Enjoy Scenic Drives – From the rolling hills of Tuscany to the Amalfi Coast's winding roads, the journey itself is an experience.

✅ Savor Local Culture – Stop at family-run trattorias, local wineries, and artisan shops for authentic experiences.

Planning ahead ensures you make the most of your time, avoid unnecessary stress, and create an itinerary that balances adventure, relaxation, and cultural immersion.

How to Use This Atlas Effectively

Embarking on a road trip through Italy is an exciting adventure, but to make the most of your journey, it's essential to have the right tools at your fingertips. Italy Atlas Road Map 2025 is designed to be your ultimate road trip companion, providing everything you need for smooth navigation, efficient planning, and an enriched travel experience.

This guide isn't just about maps—it's about creating an immersive journey. Whether you're planning a long cross-country trip or a short weekend escape, knowing how to use this atlas will ensure that every mile you drive is filled with exploration, culture, and unforgettable moments.

Maximizing the Use of This Atlas

This book is structured to help you plan, navigate, and experience Italy with ease. To get the most out of it, follow these steps:

1. Understanding the Layout

The atlas is divided into several key sections to make your journey seamless:

📍 Regional Overviews – Each chapter covers different regions of Italy, highlighting major cities, hidden gems, and must-visit attractions.

📍 Road Maps & Route Suggestions – Detailed maps include highways, scenic byways, and alternative routes to avoid traffic congestion.

📍 Travel Essentials – Information on toll roads, gas stations, parking, and local driving laws to keep you well-prepared.

📍 Cultural Insights – Learn about each region's history, food, and customs to enhance your travel experience.

📍 Accommodations & Dining – Suggested hotels, agriturismi (farm stays), and restaurants to enjoy authentic Italian hospitality.

2. Planning Your Itinerary

Rather than just following a map, use this guide to craft an itinerary that suits your travel style:

✅ Short Road Trips (3-5 Days) – Ideal for exploring a single region in depth (e.g., Tuscany, Amalfi Coast).

✅ Medium-Length Adventures (7-10 Days) – Perfect for covering multiple regions (e.g., Rome to Florence to Venice).

✅ Grand Tours (14+ Days) – Experience the full spectrum of Italy, from north to south, including islands like Sicily and Sardinia.

Each itinerary suggestion includes estimated driving times, must-see attractions, and recommended detours for an off-the-beaten-path experience.

3. Navigating the Road Maps

The maps in this atlas are designed to provide clarity and accuracy:

🚗 Color-Coded Routes – Easily identify major highways, scenic routes, and secondary roads.

🚗 Icons & Landmarks – Locate fuel stations, rest stops, scenic viewpoints, and historical sites.

🚗 Traffic & Weather Tips – Understand the best seasons and times for driving in different regions.

Using these maps in combination with GPS navigation (Google Maps, Waze, or in-car systems) will keep you on track while allowing for spontaneity.

Essential Road Trip Tips and Driving Etiquette in Italy

Driving in Italy can be an absolute joy—imagine cruising along vineyard-covered hills in Tuscany or hugging the cliffs of the Amalfi Coast with the Mediterranean shimmering below. However, Italian roads also come with their own unique challenges and customs, which is why understanding local driving etiquette is crucial.

1. General Driving Rules in Italy

Before hitting the road, familiarize yourself with these fundamental regulations:

☐ Drive on the Right – Like most of Europe, Italy follows right-hand driving.

☐ Seatbelts Are Mandatory – All passengers must wear seatbelts at all times.

☐ Speed Limits Are Strictly Enforced – Italy has many speed cameras (Autovelox), so always adhere to posted limits.

☐ Zero Tolerance for Drinking & Driving – The legal blood alcohol limit is 0.05%, and for new drivers (less than 3 years of experience), it's 0.00%.

☐ No Handheld Phones – You must use hands-free devices if making a call while driving.

2. Understanding Speed Limits

The kind of road determines the speed limit:

☐☐ 130 km/h (80 mph) – On autostrade (highways), unless there's bad weather, then it's 110 km/h (68 mph).

☐☐ 110 km/h (68 mph) – On major regional roads outside cities.

☐☐ 90 km/h (56 mph) – On secondary roads.

☐☐ 50 km/h (31 mph) – In towns and city centers.

⚠☐ Tip: Speed cameras are everywhere, and fines can be mailed internationally if you're driving a rental car

3. Tolls and Payment Systems

Most major highways (autostrade) in Italy are toll roads, and you'll need to be prepared for payment.

☐ Telepass – An electronic toll collection system that allows you to drive through without stopping. Ideal for long trips.

☐ Cash & Credit Card Payments – Most toll booths accept credit/debit cards and cash.

☐ Ticket System – When entering a highway, take a ticket; pay the toll when you exit.

⚠☐ Tip: If you lose your ticket, you'll be charged the highest possible toll fare!

4. Parking in Italy

Finding parking can be a challenge in historic city centers, so keep these tips in mind:

🅿 White Lines – Free parking (rare in major cities).

🅿 Blue Lines – Paid parking (use machines or mobile apps).

🅿 Yellow Lines – Reserved for residents or disabled drivers.

Many cities have ZTL (Zona a Traffico Limitato) zones, where non-resident vehicles are not allowed to enter without a permit. Driving into a ZTL without authorization results in a hefty fine.

5. Italian Driving Etiquette

Italians are known for their passionate driving style. Here's how to blend in:

✅ Use Your Horn (But Not Excessively) – It's common to honk when approaching tight turns or alerting slower drivers.

✅ Flash Headlights as a Warning – On highways, if a car behind you flashes its lights, it's a signal to move over.

✅ Roundabouts Have Right of Way – Entering vehicles must yield to traffic already in the roundabout.

✅ Lane Discipline – The left lane on highways is strictly for passing. If you linger, expect tailgating!

Overview of Italy's Road Infrastructure and Key Highways

Italy's road network is one of the best in Europe, combining modern highways with scenic country roads.

1. Types of Roads in Italy

🚗 Autostrade (Highways) – High-speed, well-maintained toll roads connecting major cities (prefix "A").

🚗 Strade Statali (State Roads) – Smaller but still major roads (prefix "SS").

🚗 Strade Provinciali (Provincial Roads) – Rural and scenic routes (prefix "SP").

🚗 Local & Historic Roads – Narrow, winding roads found in countryside and older towns.

2. Key Highways to Know

☐ A1 (Autostrada del Sole) – Connects Milan, Florence, Rome, and Naples (Italy's main north-south highway).

☐ A4 (Turin to Trieste) – A major east-west route passing through Venice and Verona.

☐ A14 (Adriatic Coast Highway) – Runs along Italy's eastern coastline from Bologna to Bari.

☐ A22 (Brenner Pass Highway) – The main route connecting Italy to Austria and Germany.

☐ SS163 (Amalfi Coast Road) – One of the most scenic drives in the world.

CHAPTER ONE

Understanding Italy's Road System

Italy boasts one of the most extensive and efficient road networks in Europe, seamlessly connecting major cities, picturesque countryside villages, and breathtaking coastal regions. Whether you're zipping down a high-speed Autostrada, taking the scenic route on a Strada Provinciale, or maneuvering through historic town centers on narrow local roads, understanding Italy's road system is is necessary for a comfortable and enjoyable ride.

This chapter will break down Italy's road classifications, helping you navigate like a pro and maximize the efficiency and safety of your road trip.

Italy's Road Classifications

Italy's road system is hierarchically structured, meaning different types of roads serve different purposes, from high-speed travel to slow, scenic detours. Below are the main road classifications you'll encounter on your journey:

Road Type   Purpose Speed Limit   Toll System?

Autostrade (A)   High-speed motorways, intercity travel   130 km/h (80 mph)   Yes (mostly)

Strade Statali (SS)   Major state roads, regional connectors   90-110 km/h (56-68 mph) No

Strade Provinciali (SP)   Smaller provincial roads, scenic routes 70-90 km/h (43-56 mph)   No

Local Roads   City streets, historic town roads 30-50 km/h (18-31 mph)   No

Let's break these down in detail.

1. Autostrade (Motorways) – High-Speed Expressways

The Autostrade (plural of Autostrada) are Italy's fastest and most direct routes, designed to connect major cities and regions. Comparable to Germany's Autobahn or the U.S. Interstate system, these roads are multi-lane highways that allow for high-speed travel but often require toll payments.

Key Features of the Autostrade:

✓ Wide, well-maintained highways with multiple lanes.

✓ Limited access with designated entry and exit points.

✓ Toll-based system (with a few exceptions).

✓ Service areas (Aree di Servizio) every 30-50 km for fuel, food, and rest stops.

✓ Speed limit: 130 km/h (80 mph) in good weather, reduced to 110 km/h (68 mph) in rain or fog.

How the Toll System Works

Most Autostrade are toll roads, meaning you'll need to pay to use them. Payment is based on the distance traveled, and you can pay in three ways:

♦ Cash or Credit Card – Take a ticket when entering and pay at the exit.

♦ Telepass – A pre-paid electronic toll device that allows fast, contactless payments (ideal for long trips).

♦ Viacard – A pre-loaded toll payment card available at gas stations and service areas.

Major Autostrade to Know:

☐ A1 (Autostrada del Sole) – The longest and most important motorway, connecting Milan, Bologna, Florence, Rome, and Naples.

☐ A4 – Runs east-west from Turin to Trieste, passing through Milan, Venice, and Verona.

☐ A14 (Adriatic Highway) – Stretches along Italy's eastern coast, linking Bologna to Bari.

☐ A22 (Brenner Pass Highway) – Connects Italy to Austria, a major route for those heading north.

☐ A3 (Naples to Calabria) – A crucial link to the southern regions, including the Amalfi Coast.

⚠☐ Tip: Speeding on the Autostrade is monitored by Tutor speed cameras, which track your average speed over long distances, not just at specific points. Fines are mailed internationally if you're driving a rental car.

2. Strade Statali (SS) – Major State Roads

The Strade Statali (SS) are Italy's primary state roads, serving as regional connectors between cities and towns. These roads are free to use and provide alternatives to toll highways, though they may take longer due to traffic lights, lower speed limits, and fewer lanes.

Key Features of Strade Statali:

✅ No tolls, making them a budget-friendly alternative.

✅ Speed limits range from 90-110 km/h (56-68 mph).

✅ Generally well-maintained but may have more local traffic.

✅ Great for scenic detours if you want to avoid highways.

Major Strade Statali to Know:

☐ SS1 (Via Aurelia) – A stunning coastal road following the Ligurian and Tuscan coastline.

☐ SS16 (Adriatic Road) – A slower but scenic route along the east coast.

☐ SS163 (Amalfi Coast Road) – One of the most breathtaking but challenging roads, famous for its tight curves and ocean views.

⚠️ Tip: While SS roads are generally less crowded than highways, be prepared for local traffic, cyclists, and frequent roundabouts.

3. Strade Provinciali (SP) – Scenic Provincial Roads

The Strade Provinciali (SP) are provincial roads that wind through Italy's countryside, vineyards, and mountains. If you're looking for a picturesque road trip, this is where the magic happens.

Key Features of Strade Provinciali:

✅ Great for exploring rural areas and hidden gems.

✅ Lower speed limits (70-90 km/h or 43-56 mph).

✅ Often narrower and curvier than SS roads.

✅ Less traffic, but you might encounter slow-moving farm vehicles.

Famous Scenic SP Roads:

☐ SP438 (Crete Senesi, Tuscany) – A rolling landscape of golden fields and cypress-lined roads.

☐ SP65 (Futa Pass, Emilia-Romagna) – A historic mountain road with hairpin bends.

☐ SP71 (Chianti Wine Route) – A must-drive for wine lovers in Tuscany.

⚠️ Tip: Some SP roads are not well-maintained, especially in remote areas, so drive cautiously.

4. Local Roads – The Heart of Italian Cities and Villages

Local roads wind through historic town centers, charming coastal villages, and medieval cities. They can be narrow, cobblestoned, and tricky to navigate, especially in areas built before cars existed!

Key Features of Local Roads:

✅ Speed limits: 30-50 km/h (18-31 mph).

✅ Often pedestrian-heavy, especially in tourist areas.

✅ Parking is scarce; many areas have ZTL (limited traffic zones).

✅ One-way streets are common, so use navigation apps carefully.

⚠️ Tip: Many Italian cities have ZTL (Zona a Traffico Limitato) zones, where only residents and authorized vehicles can enter. Driving into one without a permit will result in an automatic fine.

Navigating Toll Roads, Payment Systems, and Driving Regulations in Italy

Driving through Italy offers an unforgettable experience, but understanding the country's toll roads, payment methods, and driving regulations is essential for a stress-free journey. The Italian road system, particularly its network of Autostrade (motorways), operates on a toll-based system that can be confusing if you're unfamiliar with it. Additionally, speed limits, traffic rules, and enforcement mechanisms—such as speed cameras and limited traffic zones—are strictly regulated, and violating them can result in hefty fines.

This chapter will guide you through toll payment systems like Telepass and Viacard, explain how to navigate toll booths, and outline key driving laws to keep you safe and penalty-free.

Understanding Toll Roads in Italy

The Autostrade (motorways) are Italy's fastest and most direct highways, but they require toll payments. The toll system is distance-based, meaning the farther you travel, the more you pay.

How Toll Roads Work

Entering the Autostrada:

As you approach an entry ramp, you'll see a toll booth with multiple lanes.

If you don't have an electronic payment system, take a paper ticket from the machine.

Do not lose this ticket—you will need it when you exit the highway.

Driving on the Autostrada:

There are frequent service stations (Aree di Servizio) offering fuel, food, and restrooms.

Speed limits are strictly enforced using Tutor speed cameras.

Exiting and Paying the Toll:

When you leave the Autostrada, approach the toll booth and choose the correct payment lane.

Insert your ticket into the machine, and it will calculate your fare based on your entry point.

Toll Payment Methods in Italy

Italy offers several payment options for toll roads, allowing you to choose the most convenient method for your trip.

1. Telepass – The Easiest and Fastest Option

🚗 What is Telepass?

A small electronic device that automatically deducts toll fees from a linked account.

Installed on your car's windshield and allows you to pass through toll booths without stopping.

The device beeps when your payment is registered.

✅ Advantages:

Fastest option—no need to stop at toll booths.

Works on ferries, parking lots, and some ZTL zones.

Great for frequent travelers or those renting a car for an extended trip.

How to Get Telepass:

If you're renting a car, ask the rental company for a Telepass-equipped vehicle.

If driving your own car, you can subscribe online or at Autostrade service points.

2. Viacard – Prepaid Toll Card

What is Viacard?

A prepaid card used for toll payments, available in €25, €50, or €75 denominations.

Works in lanes marked "Viacard" at toll booths.

Can be purchased at gas stations, Autogrill service areas, and banks.

Advantages:

Convenient if you don't want to use cash or credit cards.

Works in automatic toll booths.

Limitations:

If the card balance is too low to cover your toll fee, you'll have to pay the remaining amount in cash.

3. Cash and Credit Card Payments

🚗 Paying with Cash:

Available at most toll booths, but queues can be long during peak hours.

Choose a lane marked with a cash symbol (€ sign).

If the machine doesn't give change, you may need exact cash.

🚗 Paying with a Credit/Debit Card:

Choose a lane marked with the credit card symbol.

Most major cards (Visa, Mastercard, American Express) are accepted.

Speed Limits and Driving Regulations in Italy

Italy has strict speed limits and road regulations, with heavy fines for violations. Understanding these rules is crucial to avoid penalties and ensure a safe, smooth journey.

Speed Limits in Italy

Speed limits in Italy vary depending on the type of road and weather conditions:

Road Type	Normal Conditions	Rain/Fog Conditions
Autostrade (Motorways)	130 km/h (80 mph)	110 km/h (68 mph)

Strade Statali (State Roads)   110 km/h (68 mph)   90 km/h (56 mph)

Strade Provinciali (Provincial Roads)   90 km/h (56 mph)   70 km/h (43 mph)

Urban Roads (City Streets) 50 km/h (31 mph)   50 km/h (31 mph)

🚨 Important Notes:

Speed limits are reduced in rain or fog—violating these rules can lead to higher fines.

Some Autostrade allow a speed limit of 150 km/h (93 mph) in perfect weather conditions, but always check local signs.

Speed limits are strictly enforced using cameras and radar traps.

Speed Cameras and Fines

Italy uses several types of speed enforcement systems:

✅ Tutor System:

Measures average speed over long highway sections.

Unlike regular speed traps, slowing down near the camera won't help—you must maintain a legal speed throughout the monitored stretch.

✅ Autovelox (Speed Cameras):

Fixed speed cameras installed along highways and local roads.

Often signposted, but some areas use hidden cameras.

✓ Mobile Speed Traps:

Police frequently set up temporary radar traps on rural roads and highways.

🚨 What Happens If You Get a Speeding Ticket?

If you're driving a rental car, the fine will be sent to the rental company, which will charge your credit card.

Fines increase if not paid within 60 days.

Foreign drivers cannot avoid paying fines—Italian authorities work with international agencies to collect penalties.

Other Important Driving Regulations

✓ Seat Belts:

Mandatory for all passengers.

Fines apply if any passenger is not wearing a seatbelt.

✓ Alcohol Limit:

Standard blood alcohol limit: 0.05%.

For new drivers (less than 3 years of experience): 0.00%—NO alcohol allowed.

Fines for DUI can exceed €1,500, and severe cases may result in vehicle confiscation.

✅ ZTL (Limited Traffic Zones):

Many Italian cities (Rome, Florence, Milan, etc.) have restricted zones where only residents and authorized vehicles can enter.

Cameras enforce ZTL rules, and fines are automatically issued if you drive in a restricted area without permission.

✅ Right of Way:

Traffic from the right has priority unless otherwise indicated.

At crosswalks, pedestrians always have the right-of-way.

✅ Use of Headlights:

Mandatory on highways and rural roads during the day.

✅ Using a Mobile Phone:

Hands-free use only—holding your phone while driving can result in fines

Road Signs, Fuel Stations, and EV Charging Points in Italy

Navigating Italy's roads requires more than just a good map or GPS—you need to understand road signs, fuel stations, and EV charging points to ensure a smooth journey. Road signs in Italy follow international conventions, but some may be unfamiliar if you're not used to European driving standards. Additionally, knowing where to find fuel stations, what types of fuel are available, and how to locate EV charging points is essential for long trips.

In this chapter, we will explore Italy's road signage system, help you decode important traffic symbols, and provide a detailed guide on fuel stations and electric vehicle charging infrastructure.

Understanding Italian Road Signs

Italy follows the Vienna Convention on Road Signs and Signals, meaning many signs are similar to those in other European countries. However, there are some unique features and Italian-specific signs that every driver should recognize.

Categories of Italian Road Signs

Road signs in Italy are divided into five main categories, each with distinct shapes and colors:

CategoryColor & Shape   Purpose

Warning Signs   ⚠□ Triangular (Red Border, White Background) Alert drivers about hazards like sharp turns, pedestrian crossings, or steep inclines.

Regulatory Signs ● Circular (Red Border, White Background) Indicate speed limits, entry restrictions, and no-overtaking zones.

Mandatory Signs ⊜ Circular (Blue Background, White Symbol) Indicate actions that must be taken (e.g., "Turn Right," "Pedestrian Zone").

Information Signs ▢ Rectangular (Blue Background) Provide useful info like service areas, rest stops, or parking zones.

Directional Signs ▢ Green (Motorways), Blue (Main Roads), White (Local Roads) Show directions to cities, highways, and destinations.

Common Italian Road Signs and Their Meanings

⚠▢ Warning Signs (Pericolo - Danger)

These red-bordered triangular signs warn about road hazards ahead.

Curva Pericolosa (Dangerous Curve) → ⚠▢

Incrocio Pericoloso (Dangerous Intersection) → ⚠▢

Passaggio a Livello (Railway Crossing) → 🚉

Discesa Ripida / Salita Ripida (Steep Descent/Ascent) → 〰️

● Regulatory Signs (Regolamentazione - Restrictions)

These signs indicate speed limits, no-entry zones, or prohibitions.

Divieto di Accesso (No Entry) → ✖

Divieto di Sosta (No Parking) → 🅿□✖

Limite di Velocità (Speed Limit) → 🚗 50 km/h (City), 130 km/h (Autostrada)

ZTL – Zona a Traffico Limitato (Restricted Traffic Zone) → □□□

● Mandatory Signs (Obbligo - Must Follow)

These indicate required actions for drivers.

Direzione Obligatoria (Mandatory Direction) → ●←□→□↑□

Percorso Pedonale (Pedestrian Path) → 🚶♂□●

Catene da Neve Obbligatorie (Snow Chains Required) → ❄□□

□ Directional and Informational Signs

Green Signs → Autostrade (Motorways)

Blue Signs → Strade Statali (State Roads)

White Signs → Local and rural roads

Fuel Stations in Italy: Where and How to Fill Up

Whether you're driving a gasoline, diesel, or electric vehicle, knowing how to refuel or recharge in Italy is crucial for a hassle-free trip.

Types of Fuel in Italy

When pulling up to an Italian fuel station, you'll notice several types of fuel available:

Fuel Type	Italian Name	Description	Pump Color
Unleaded Petrol	Benzina Senza Piombo	(95 or 98 octane) Standard gasoline fuel	Green
Diesel	Gasolio	Common for European cars and trucks	Black/Yellow
LPG (Liquefied Petroleum Gas)	GPL (Gas di Petrolio Liquefatto)	Alternative fuel for some vehicles	Blue
Methane (CNG)	Metano	Available in select locations	Orange

🚨 Warning: Diesel and gasoline nozzles may fit into the same tank opening! Double-check before refueling.

How to Refuel Your Car in Italy

Full-Service ("Servito") or Self-Service ("Fai da te")?

Some stations offer full service where an attendant fills your tank, while others are self-service.

Self-service is cheaper (around €0.10–€0.15 less per liter).

Paying for Fuel

You can pay at the pump with cash, credit/debit card, or pre-paid fuel cards.

In remote areas, pumps may require prepayment via a cash machine.

Fuel Availability and Opening Hours

Most Autostrade stations are open 24/7.

Rural stations may close for lunch (1:00 PM – 3:30 PM) and on Sundays.

Electric Vehicle (EV) Charging in Italy

Italy is rapidly expanding its electric vehicle infrastructure, making road trips in an EV more feasible than ever.

Types of EV Chargers in Italy

Charging Type	Speed	Time to Charge (Full)	Best For
AC Standard Charging (Type 2)	3–22 kW	4–8 hours	Overnight charging
DC Fast Charging (CHAdeMO, CCS)	50 kW	1–2 hours	Highways & cities
Ultra-Fast Charging (Ionity, Tesla Supercharger)	150+ kW	30 min – 1 hour	Long-distance travel

🚘 Popular Charging Networks:

Enel X (JuicePass) – Most extensive network

Ionity – Ultra-fast charging on highways

Tesla Superchargers – Exclusive for Tesla vehicles

🚨 Key EV Travel Tips:

Use apps like PlugShare, Enel X JuicePass, or Tesla Maps to locate chargers.

Some rural areas lack high-speed charging—plan accordingly.

Bring an adapter for Type 2 charging stations if needed.

ITALY

CHAPTER TWO

Planning Your Italian Road Trip

Embarking on a road trip across Italy is an unforgettable experience filled with breathtaking landscapes, rich history, and mouthwatering cuisine. However, choosing the right time to travel can make all the difference in your adventure. From navigating peak tourist seasons to finding the perfect weather for scenic drives, proper planning will ensure your journey is as enjoyable and stress-free as possible.

In this chapter, we'll explore the best times of the year for a road trip, considering factors such as climate, crowds, and regional events.

Best Times of the Year for a Road Trip in Italy

Italy is a country of four distinct seasons, each offering unique experiences for travelers. While some months bring ideal weather and fewer tourists, others may come with heavy traffic, closed attractions, or extreme temperatures. Let's break down the pros and cons of each season to help you decide the perfect time for your road trip.

Spring (March – May) 🌸🚗

Why Go?

Mild temperatures (15°C–22°C / 59°F–72°F) – perfect for driving and sightseeing.

Flowers in full bloom—Tuscany's rolling hills and Sicily's countryside look stunning.

Fewer tourists compared to summer, making popular destinations more enjoyable.

Things to Consider:

Higher chance of rain in March and April.

Some mountain passes in the Alps and Dolomites may still be closed due to snow.

Easter (Pasqua) can bring heavy crowds, especially in Rome, Florence, and Venice.

💡 Spring Road Trip Idea:

Drive through Tuscany and Umbria to witness vibrant green landscapes and charming medieval villages in their full bloom.

Summer (June – August) ☀️ □□□🚗

Why Go?

Long daylight hours—drive and explore until late evening.

Perfect for coastal road trips along the Amalfi Coast, Cinque Terre, or Puglia.

Vibrant festivals and events, including Palio di Siena and Festa della Madonna Bruna.

Things to Consider:

Peak tourist season—crowded cities, beaches, and higher accommodation prices.

Extreme heat, especially in Rome, Florence, and southern Italy (often exceeding 35°C / 95°F).

Traffic congestion, particularly on highways leading to coastal towns.

💡 Summer Road Trip Idea:

Take a scenic drive along the Amalfi Coast, enjoying sea breezes, fresh seafood, and picturesque cliffside villages.

Autumn (September – November) 🍂🚗

Why Go?

Mild temperatures (18°C–24°C / 64°F–75°F)—ideal for outdoor activities and road trips.

Grape harvest season—perfect for visiting vineyards in Tuscany, Piedmont, and Sicily.

Fewer crowds compared to summer, making it easier to book accommodations.

Things to Consider:

Rainfall increases in October and November, especially in northern regions.

Some tourist services start to close in late autumn, particularly in small coastal towns.

💡 **Autumn Road Trip Idea:**

Tour the Langhe wine region in Piedmont, experiencing the grape harvest and tasting world-famous Barolo wines.

Winter (December – February) ❄ ☐☐☐ 🚗

Why Go?

Magical winter landscapes, especially in the Dolomites and the Alps.

Christmas markets in cities like Rome, Milan, and Florence.

Lower accommodation prices (except during holiday periods).

Things to Consider:

Snow and ice can make mountain driving difficult—chains or winter tires may be required.

Many coastal and rural attractions close during the low season.

Shorter daylight hours, meaning less time for driving and sightseeing.

💡 **Winter Road Trip Idea:**

Explore the Italian Alps and Dolomites, enjoying skiing, cozy mountain villages, and breathtaking snowy scenery.

Verdict: When is the Best Time to Road Trip in Italy?

Season   Best For Weather Crowds

Spring (March–May) Flower-filled landscapes, fewer tourists ☐☐ Mild☺ Moderate

Summer (June–August) Coastal drives, beach towns, festivals ☀☐ Hot ☐ Very High

Autumn (September–November) Wine regions, mild weather, scenic countryside 🍃 Cool ☐ Moderate

Winter (December–February) Alpine routes, Christmas markets, skiing ❄☐ Cold ☐☐ Low (except for ski areas)

🚗 Final Recommendation:

For mild weather, fewer tourists, and stunning landscapes, spring (April–May) and autumn (September–October) are the best times for a road trip in Italy. If you want beach adventures and lively summer vibes, then June is ideal before peak crowds arrive.

Choosing the Right Vehicle: Car Rental, Camper Van, or Personal Car

Selecting the right vehicle is a crucial decision when planning a road trip through Italy. The country's diverse landscapes, ranging from narrow medieval streets to expansive highways, require careful consideration of what type of vehicle will best suit your journey. Should you rent a car, opt for a camper van, or drive your own personal vehicle? Every option has benefits and drawbacks of its own. In this section, we'll explore the best options to help you make an informed decision.

1. Renting a Car in Italy: Pros, Cons, and Tips 🚗

For most travelers, renting a car is the most convenient way to explore Italy's roads. It offers flexibility, comfort, and the ability to customize your itinerary.

✅ Pros of Renting a Car

✔☐ Convenience – Pick up and drop off at major airports, train stations, and city centers.

✔☐ Fuel Efficiency – Rental companies offer modern cars with good fuel economy.

✔☐ Wide Selection – Choose from compact cars, SUVs, or luxury vehicles.

✔☐ Cross-Border Options – Some companies allow driving to neighboring countries like France, Switzerland, and Austria.

✖ Cons of Renting a Car

✖ Rental Costs – Prices vary based on season, location, and vehicle type.

✖ Insurance Fees – Basic insurance is included, but extra coverage can be expensive.

✖ Limited Access in ZTL Zones – Many Italian cities have restricted traffic zones (ZTL) where rental cars are prohibited.

☐ Best Car Rental Companies in Italy

Avis, Hertz, and Europcar – Reliable international brands with multiple locations.

AutoEurope – A great platform for comparing prices.

Locauto and Sicily by Car – Good local rental companies with competitive rates.

💡 Pro Tips for Renting a Car in Italy

♦ Book Early – Prices increase closer to travel dates.

♦ Get a Small Car – Ideal for navigating narrow streets and tight parking spots.

♦ Manual vs. Automatic – Automatics are more expensive; manual cars are common.

♦ Check for ZTL Areas – Avoid fines by understanding restricted zones in cities.

♦ Inspect Before Driving – Take photos of any damage before leaving the rental lot.

2. Traveling by Camper Van: The Ultimate Road Trip Experience ☐

For those who want total freedom, a camper van or motorhome is a fantastic way to explore Italy. It allows you to stay in nature, save on hotel costs, and travel at your own pace.

✅ Pros of a Camper Van

✅ No Need for Hotels – Sleep wherever camping is allowed.

✅ Flexibility – Adjust plans without worrying about accommodation bookings.

✅ Perfect for Remote Areas – Explore rural Tuscany, Dolomites, and coastal regions.

✅ Great for Families and Groups – More space and comfort than a car.

❌ Cons of a Camper Van

❌ Higher Fuel Costs – Camper vans consume more fuel than regular cars.

❌ Restricted Parking – Many Italian cities do not allow camper vans in central areas.

❌ Road Challenges – Some mountain passes and historic villages have roads too narrow for large campers.

❌ Camping Restrictions – You can't park overnight everywhere; designated campsites are required.

◻ Best Camper Van Rental Companies in Italy

Indie Campers – Offers fully equipped vans and motorhomes.

McRent – Reliable for large motorhome rentals.

Yescapa – A peer-to-peer camper rental platform with affordable options.

🔥 Pro Tips for Camper Van Travel

♦ Plan Campsites in Advance – Wild camping is illegal in most areas. Use sites like Campercontact or Park4Night.

♦ Avoid Big Cities – Park outside urban areas and use public transport to visit city centers.

♦ Check for Low-Emission Zones – Some Italian cities restrict older diesel vehicles.

3. Driving Your Personal Car: When Is It the Best Choice? 🚙

If you're traveling from a nearby country (France, Switzerland, Austria, or Slovenia), driving your own car can be a great option. However, if you're coming from overseas, bringing your own car is rarely practical due to shipping costs and logistics.

✅ Pros of Using Your Own Car

✓◻ No Rental Costs – Save money on daily rental fees.

✓☐ **Familiarity** – Drive a car you already know and are comfortable with.

✓☐ **More Packing Space** – No restrictions on luggage weight or size.

✘ **Cons of Using Your Own Car**

✘ **Long Drives to Reach Italy** – Can be tiring if you're coming from distant parts of Europe.

✘ **Wear and Tear** – Long journeys may cause maintenance issues.

✘ **Italian Driving Laws** – Foreign cars must have valid insurance and a vignette if required.

🔥 **Pro Tips for Using Your Own Car**

♦ **Check Insurance Coverage** – Ensure your policy includes international road travel.

♦ **Have the Right Documents** – Bring your vehicle registration, insurance, and green card.

♦ **Buy a Toll Pass (Telepass)** – Avoid queues at toll booths.

Parking in Italy: Rules, Apps, and Best Practices 🅿️

Parking in Italy, especially in historic cities, can be challenging and expensive. Understanding parking regulations and using the right apps can save you from frustration and fines.

Understanding Parking Zones

▫ White Lines – Free public parking (but often limited to residents).

▫ Blue Lines – Paid parking (rates vary by location).

▫ Yellow Lines – Reserved for disabled drivers and official vehicles.

▫ ZTL Zones – No entry for unauthorized vehicles.

💡 Top Parking Tips

✓ Park Outside the City – In major cities like Rome, Florence, and Milan, it's easier to park in suburban areas and take public transport.

✓ Use Park-and-Ride (Parcheggi di Scambio) – These lots offer cheap or free parking with metro/bus connections.

✓ Avoid Parking in ZTL Areas – Many tourists receive hefty fines for mistakenly entering restricted zones.

📱 Best Parking Apps for Italy

1️⃣ EasyPark – Works in most Italian cities, allowing cashless payments.

2️⃣ MyCicero – Good for finding and reserving spots in advance.

3️⃣ Parkopedia – Shows available parking spaces with pricing details.

4️⃣ Parclick – Offers discounts for long-term parking.

Final Thoughts: What's the Best Choice?

Vehicle Type	Best For	Pros	Cons
Rental Car 🚗	Most travelers	Easy to rent, fuel-efficient, flexible	ZTL restrictions, insurance costs
Camper Van 🚐	Adventure lovers	No hotel costs, ultimate freedom	Expensive fuel, parking restrictions
Personal Car 🚙	Nearby travelers	No rental fees, more luggage space	Insurance & paperwork required

🚗 Final Recommendation:

For urban and countryside exploration, a small rental car is the best option.

For an immersive road trip with maximum flexibility, a camper van is ideal.

If you live in Europe, using your own car can save money and add comfort.

Budgeting for Tolls, Fuel, and Accommodations

A successful road trip across Italy requires careful budgeting for essential travel costs. Whether you're cruising down the Autostrade (motorways) or exploring hidden gems in the countryside, having a clear understanding of the expenses you'll encounter—such as tolls, fuel, and accommodation— is key to making your journey smooth and enjoyable. In this section, we'll break down the typical costs and offer tips on how to keep your budget in check while enjoying the best that Italy has to offer.

Tolls in Italy: What to Expect and How to Budget

Italy has an extensive network of toll roads, primarily consisting of Autostrade (motorways). Most of these roads require toll payments, either at toll booths or via electronic payment systems.

How Tolls Work in Italy

Toll Points: On the Autostrade, you'll encounter toll booths that charge based on the distance traveled or type of vehicle. The toll system is managed by Autostrade per l'Italia and other regional operators.

Payment Methods:

Cash: Available at most toll booths, but expect a longer wait time during busy travel periods.

Credit Cards: Most booths accept major credit cards (Visa, MasterCard).

Telepass: A convenient electronic system for automatic toll payment. Simply drive through dedicated lanes without stopping.

Viacard: A preloaded card that can be used at toll booths.

Toll Pricing

Toll costs can vary depending on several factors, including the length of your journey, the vehicle type, and the region. For example, traveling from Milan to Rome on the A1 Autostrada can cost around €40-€50 for a standard car. Shorter routes or less popular highways are often cheaper.

Average Cost: A journey of around 100-200 km can cost between €10 and €20.

Special Routes: Some mountain roads or scenic routes, like the Great Dolomite Road, may have additional tolls.

💡 Pro Tip: Consider using Telepass or a Viacard to save time and hassle at toll booths, especially during peak travel seasons.

Fuel Costs in Italy

Italy's fuel prices are known to be higher than average compared to other European countries. However, with some planning and a few tips, you can manage your fuel budget efficiently.

Current Fuel Prices

As of 2025, fuel prices in Italy are typically:

Petrol (Benzina): Around €1.70 – €2.00 per liter

Diesel (Gasolio): Around €1.50 – €1.80 per liter

Fuel prices fluctuate throughout the year, often rising in the summer months due to increased demand.

Where to Buy Fuel

Service Stations: You'll find fuel stations on highways, in cities, and along rural roads. Many of them offer both self-service and attended pumps.

Supermarkets and Discount Stations: Some supermarkets (like Coop or Esselunga) have fuel stations that offer slightly lower prices.

Motorway Rest Stops: Stations on the Autostrade tend to be more expensive than those off the motorway.

💡 Pro Tip: Fill up before entering highways or more remote areas to avoid paying premium prices at service stations along the way.

Fuel Efficiency Tips

Drive Smoothly: Avoid heavy acceleration and braking.

Keep Your Tires Inflated: Properly inflated tires can improve fuel economy.

Avoid Excessive Weight: Too much luggage or roof boxes will reduce fuel efficiency.

Accommodations in Italy: How to Budget for Stays

Italy offers a wide range of accommodations to suit every budget, from luxurious hotels to affordable B&Bs and charming agriturismos (country guesthouses). When planning your road trip, it's important to allocate funds for overnight stays, keeping in mind both your route and personal preferences.

Types of Accommodations

Hotels: From 3-star hotels to 5-star luxury resorts, Italy offers a wide range of hotel options. Prices vary significantly depending on location (e.g., Rome or Venice vs. rural areas).

Airbnb: A great option for those seeking a more personalized experience. Prices are competitive, and you can find apartments, cottages, or rooms in various settings.

Agriturismo: Staying on a farm or vineyard is a great way to experience Italy's rural charm. These accommodations often include home-cooked meals and can be more affordable than hotels.

Hostels: For budget travelers, hostels are available in major cities and popular tourist destinations. They offer shared rooms and cheap rates.

Average Costs

Budget Accommodation: Expect to pay around €50-€100 per night for basic accommodations such as hostels, B&Bs, or guesthouses.

Mid-Range Accommodation: For a comfortable hotel or private Airbnb, expect to pay around €100-€200 per night.

Luxury Accommodation: Prices for high-end hotels can exceed €300 per night in major cities and popular tourist spots.

Booking Tips

Book Early: Accommodation costs rise during peak season (especially in Rome, Venice, and Florence). Book your stays in advance to lock in better rates.

Stay Outside City Centers: If you don't mind a short drive or public transport commute, staying in suburban areas can save you money.

Consider Agriturismos: These country stays offer a local experience and tend to be more affordable than urban hotels.

Road Safety and Emergency Contact Numbers

When driving in Italy, it's important to stay alert and aware of local road safety laws. Having a plan in case of emergencies is also crucial for your peace of mind during your trip. Here's everything you need to know to stay safe on Italy's roads.

Driving Safety Tips

Speed Limits:

Autostrade: 130 km/h (81 mph) on highways (110 km/h in wet conditions).

Secondary Roads: 90 km/h (56 mph).

Urban Areas: 50 km/h (31 mph), unless otherwise indicated.

Drink Driving: Italy has strict drink driving laws. A blood alcohol content of 0.5 grams per liter is the legal limit. For new drivers, the limit is zero.

Seatbelts: Mandatory for all passengers in both the front and back seats.

Mobile Phones: Using a mobile phone while driving is only allowed if you have a hands-free device.

Parking: Always ensure you park legally. Avoid parking in ZTL zones, as fines are hefty.

Emergency Contact Numbers

Emergency Services (Police, Ambulance, Fire): 112 (EU-wide emergency number)

Roadside Assistance: 803116 (AA or similar roadside services)

Car Rental Emergency: Contact the rental agency's emergency number if your vehicle breaks down or if you're involved in an accident.

💡 Pro Tip: Always keep your rental agreement and important contact details handy, especially if you're renting a car or camper van.

Budgeting for a Smooth Road Trip

Category	Estimated Cost	Tips
Tolls	€10–€50 per journey	Use Telepass for faster toll payments.
Fuel	€1.50–€2.00 per liter	Fill up before highways and use discount stations.
Accommodation	€50–€300 per night	Book early and consider agriturismos for savings.
Emergency Services	Free in case of emergencies	Save emergency numbers on your phone.

By planning your budget for tolls, fuel, and accommodation in advance, and understanding Italy's road safety guidelines, you'll be able to enjoy your road trip with confidence and ease.

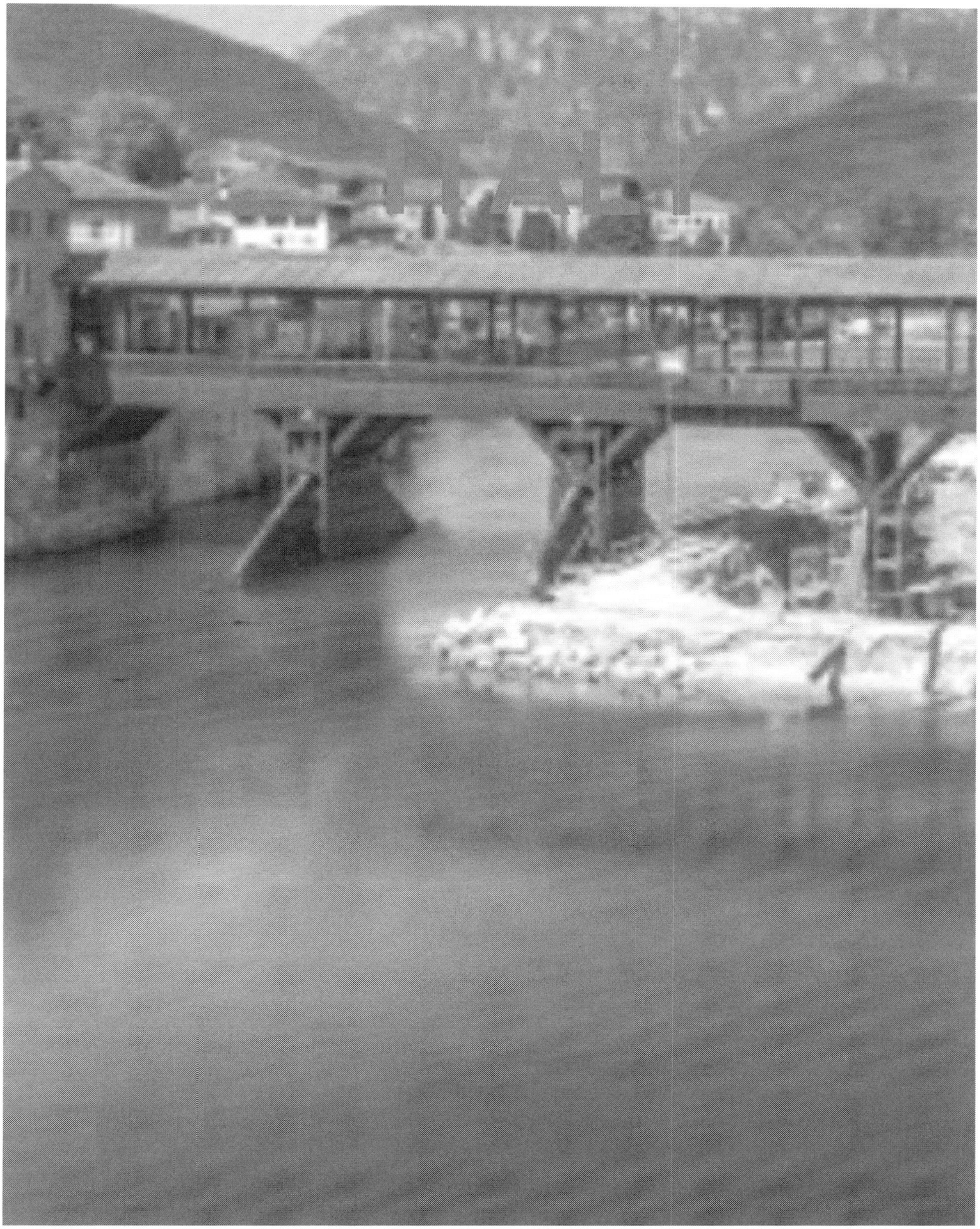

CHAPTER THREE

Northern Italy Road Trips

The Italian Alps and Dolomites Scenic Route

Italy's northern regions are home to some of the most spectacular mountain landscapes in the world. The Italian Alps and Dolomites offer a road trip filled with towering peaks, alpine lakes, charming villages, and thrilling winding roads. Whether you're an adventure seeker looking for hiking trails and ski resorts or a leisurely traveler craving breathtaking scenery and cultural experiences, this scenic route delivers an once-in-a-lifetime experience.

Exploring the Breathtaking Mountain Landscapes

Why Choose This Route?

Driving through the Italian Alps and Dolomites is an experience like no other. The dramatic peaks, winding roads, and picturesque valleys make it a bucket-list-worthy road trip. Here's what makes this route so special:

✓ World-Famous Scenic Drives: Roads like the Great Dolomite Road and Passo dello Stelvio provide some of the most stunning panoramas in Europe.

✓ Charming Alpine Villages: Stops in places like Cortina d'Ampezzo, Bolzano, and Bressanone let you experience local culture, traditional food, and cozy mountain lodges.

✅ Outdoor Adventures: Hiking, skiing, rock climbing, and cable car rides offer endless opportunities for adventure.

✅ Hidden Gems: Discover secret lakes, remote mountain huts, and lesser-known nature trails away from the crowds.

Best Route: The Great Dolomite Road (Strada delle Dolomiti)

📍 Distance: 110 km (68 miles)

📍 Driving Time: Approximately 3 hours (without stops)

📍 Start Point: Bolzano

📍 End Point: Cortina d'Ampezzo

📍 Best Time to Visit: Late spring to early autumn (May to October)

The Great Dolomite Road (Strada delle Dolomiti) is one of the most iconic scenic routes in Italy. It connects Bolzano to Cortina d'Ampezzo, winding through stunning mountain passes, picturesque valleys, and breathtaking viewpoints.

Key Stops Along the Route

🚗 Bolzano – Gateway to the Dolomites

Begin your journey in Bolzano, the capital of South Tyrol, where Italian and Austrian cultures blend beautifully. Visit the South Tyrol Museum of Archaeology to see Ötzi the

Iceman, a 5,300-year-old mummy found in the Alps. Stroll through the Piazza Walther and grab a cappuccino before hitting the road.

🚗 Val di Fassa – Stunning Mountain Views

Drive through the Val di Fassa, where lush green valleys meet the towering Dolomites. This area is perfect for short hikes, picnics, or taking a break at an authentic Tyrolean restaurant to try dishes like canederli (dumplings) and speck (smoked ham).

🚗 Passo Pordoi – Breathtaking Switchbacks

One of the most dramatic high-altitude roads on this route, Passo Pordoi (2,239 meters above sea level) offers hairpin turns, panoramic vistas, and excellent photography spots. Stop at the Pordoi Cable Car for a ride to the Sass Pordoi summit, which gives you 360° views of the Dolomites.

🚗 Lago di Carezza – The Emerald Lake

This magical alpine lake, known as the "Rainbow Lake," reflects the jagged peaks of the Latemar mountains. A quick 30-minute stop here is enough to enjoy its beauty and snap a few breathtaking pictures.

🚗 Cortina d'Ampezzo – The Jewel of the Dolomites

Your journey ends in Cortina d'Ampezzo, a famous ski and mountain resort town known for its elegant boutiques, lively après-ski scene, and luxurious chalets. If visiting in winter, enjoy skiing and snowboarding; in summer, go for hiking and mountain biking.

💡 Pro Tip: If you have extra time, take a detour to Tre Cime di Lavaredo, one of the most famous mountain formations in the Dolomites, ideal for a scenic hike.

Alternative Route: The Stelvio Pass (Passo dello Stelvio)

📍 Distance: 75 km (47 miles)

📍 Driving Time: Approximately 2-3 hours

📍 Start Point: Bormio

📍 End Point: Merano

📍 Best Time to Visit: June to September (closed in winter due to snow)

For thrill-seekers, the Stelvio Pass is one of the most challenging and rewarding roads in Europe. With 48 hairpin turns, it's a dream drive for motorcyclists and sports car enthusiasts.

Key Highlights of Stelvio Pass

Dramatic Elevation: Reaching 2,757 meters (9,045 feet), this is the second-highest paved road in the Alps.

Biking Paradise: Popular among cyclists who want to test their endurance on steep ascents.

Scenic Views: Every turn offers jaw-dropping panoramas of snow-capped peaks and lush valleys.

Nearby Attractions: Visit Glorenza, a charming medieval town with well-preserved walls, or relax in the Merano Thermal Baths after a long drive.

Where to Stay Along the Route

🏠 Budget Option:

Hostel Bolzano (Bolzano) – Affordable rooms in the heart of South Tyrol.

🏠 Mid-Range:

Hotel Lago di Braies (near Lago di Braies) – A cozy stay by one of the most scenic lakes in Italy.

🏠 Luxury:

Cristallo, a Luxury Collection Resort & Spa (Cortina d'Ampezzo) – Perfect for those who want stunning views and high-end comfort.

What to Pack for a Dolomites Road Trip?

✓☐ Warm Layers – Even in summer, mountain temperatures can drop quickly.

✓☐ Hiking Shoes – Many viewpoints require short hikes.

✓☐ Sunglasses & Sunscreen – High altitudes mean strong sun exposure.

✓☐ Camera – The landscapes are too beautiful not to capture!

✓☐ Snacks & Water – Some areas have limited shops, so be prepared.

A Road Trip Like No Other

A road trip through the Italian Alps and Dolomites is a journey through one of the most stunning landscapes in Europe. Whether you're looking for adventure, relaxation, or cultural experiences, this route has something for everyone.

🚘 Drive the Great Dolomite Road for incredible mountain views

🚘 Take on the Stelvio Pass if you're up for a thrilling challenge

🚘 Stop in charming villages for authentic Italian-Alpine culture

🚘 Hike, ski, or simply enjoy the breathtaking scenery

With its jaw-dropping beauty, world-class outdoor activities, and rich history, Northern Italy's mountain roads are a must-visit for any road trip enthusiast. So, fuel up your car, set your GPS, and get ready for an unforgettable Alpine adventure! ☐☐🚘✨

Must-Visit Spots: Exploring Northern Italy's Alpine Gems

A road trip through the Italian Alps and Dolomites is an experience like no other, but to truly make the most of it, you'll want to stop at some of the most stunning and culturally rich destinations along the way. These locations offer a perfect blend of natural beauty, outdoor adventure, and local charm.

1. Cortina d'Ampezzo: The Queen of the Dolomites

📍 Location: Veneto region, nestled in the heart of the Dolomites

☐ Best for: Luxury ski resorts, alpine hikes, scenic cable car rides

Cortina d'Ampezzo is one of Italy's most famous mountain towns, known for its stunning scenery, world-class ski resorts, and vibrant après-ski culture. Whether you visit in winter for skiing or summer for hiking, this charming town is a must-stop on your Dolomites road trip.

Top Things to Do in Cortina d'Ampezzo

☐ Ride the Faloria Cable Car – Enjoy panoramic views over the entire town and surrounding peaks.

⛷ Ski in the 2026 Winter Olympics host area – Cortina is set to host events during the upcoming Milan-Cortina Winter Olympics.

☐☐ Stroll along Corso Italia – The town's main shopping street, filled with high-end boutiques and cozy cafés.

☐ Hike to Lago di Sorapis – A breathtaking turquoise lake that requires a moderate 2-3 hour hike.

💡 Pro Tip: If you're visiting in winter, book your accommodations early as Cortina is a popular destination for Italian and international tourists.

2. Val Gardena: A Hidden Paradise in the Dolomites

📍 Location: South Tyrol region, in the heart of the Dolomites

☐ Best for: Traditional Alpine villages, adventure sports, breathtaking landscapes

Val Gardena is a picture-perfect valley surrounded by towering peaks and dotted with charming villages. It's a hiker's paradise in summer and a skiing wonderland in winter, making it a top destination year-round.

Must-See Villages in Val Gardena

🏠 Ortisei: The cultural heart of the valley, known for its woodcarving tradition and colorful buildings.

🏠 Santa Cristina: A smaller, quieter village, perfect for those who love authentic Alpine experiences.

🏠 Selva di Val Gardena: A lively town with access to some of the best ski slopes and hiking trails in the Dolomites.

Outdoor Adventures in Val Gardena

☐ Ride the Seceda Cable Car – One of the most iconic panoramic viewpoints in the Dolomites.

☐ Hike the Adolf Munkel Trail – A scenic walk through majestic rock formations and lush meadows.

☐☐ Ski the Sellaronda – A famous ski circuit connecting four Dolomite passes.

☐ Try Mountain Biking – Some of Italy's best cycling routes pass through Val Gardena.

💡 Pro Tip: Visit in late September or early October to witness the stunning golden hues of autumn, making the valley even more picturesque.

3. Tre Cime di Lavaredo: The Crown Jewel of the Dolomites

📍 Location: Veneto region, in the Sexten Dolomites

☐ Best for: Iconic mountain peaks, world-class hiking trails, jaw-dropping landscapes

The Tre Cime di Lavaredo (Three Peaks of Lavaredo) is one of the most famous landmarks in the Dolomites. These three massive rock formations create a jaw-dropping backdrop for any outdoor enthusiast.

Best Ways to Experience Tre Cime di Lavaredo

☐ Hike the Tre Cime Loop Trail – A 9.5 km (6-mile) loop offering stunning views of the peaks from every angle.

🚗 Drive to Rifugio Auronzo – The closest point you can reach by car before hiking.

☐ Capture sunrise or sunset – The golden light on the peaks creates a spectacular glow, making it a favorite

The Lakes Region Road Trip

Touring Lake Como, Lake Garda, and Lake Maggiore

If you're looking for a road trip that combines breathtaking natural beauty, charming villages, and rich history, then exploring Italy's Lakes Region is an experience you won't want to miss. The northern lakes—Lake Como, Lake Garda, and Lake Maggiore—offer some of the most picturesque landscapes in Italy, where crystal-clear waters meet rolling hills, alpine mountains, and elegant lakeside towns.

This road trip is perfect for travelers who enjoy scenic drives, outdoor adventures, historical sites, and luxurious retreats. Whether you want to relax at a lakeside café, explore medieval castles, or take a ferry across the shimmering waters, the Lakes Region offers something for everyone.

Stop 1: Lake Como – The Jewel of Northern Italy

📍 Location: Lombardy region

☐ Best for: Romantic getaways, luxury resorts, stunning villas

Lake Como is one of Italy's most famous and exclusive destinations. Known for its charming lakeside villages, stunning villas, and dramatic mountain backdrops, it's no surprise that it's a favorite among celebrities and travelers alike.

Top Attractions at Lake Como

🏠 Bellagio – Nicknamed the "Pearl of Lake Como," this town is famous for its cobblestone streets, elegant boutiques, and stunning lake views.

🏠 Varenna – A peaceful fishing village with colorful houses and beautiful gardens.

🏠 Tremezzo – Home to Villa Carlotta, a 17th-century villa with breathtaking botanical gardens.

⛴ Take a boat tour – The best way to explore Lake Como is by ferry or private boat, stopping at the most picturesque towns along the way.

🏰 Visit Villa Balbianello – A famous filming location for movies like Star Wars: Episode II and Casino Royale.

💡 Pro Tip: The best time to visit Lake Como is during the spring (April-May) and early autumn (September-October) when the weather is perfect and the crowds are smaller.

Stop 2: Lake Garda – Italy's Largest and Most Diverse Lake

📍 Location: Between Lombardy, Veneto, and Trentino-Alto Adige regions

- Best for: Outdoor activities, medieval castles, family-friendly adventures

Lake Garda is the largest lake in Italy and offers an exciting mix of natural beauty, history, and adventure. Whether you're into hiking, water sports, or exploring charming medieval villages, Lake Garda has something for everyone.

Must-See Towns and Attractions at Lake Garda

- Sirmione – A fairytale-like town with a 13th-century castle (Scaliger Castle) and the ancient Roman ruins of Grotte di Catullo.

- Malcesine – A charming lakeside village with Monte Baldo nearby, where you can take a cable car up for panoramic mountain views.

- Limone sul Garda – A beautiful town famous for its lemon groves and scenic lakefront promenades.

- Gardaland – Italy's largest amusement park, perfect for families and thrill-seekers.

- Cycle along the Garda Bike Path – One of the most scenic cycling routes in Europe, offering unmatched views of the lake.

💡 Pro Tip: Lake Garda is a year-round destination, but June to September is best for enjoying water activities and warm weather.

Stop 3: Lake Maggiore – A Serene and Elegant Escape

📍 Location: Piedmont and Lombardy regions, extending into Switzerland

☐ Best for: Peaceful retreats, beautiful gardens, stunning islands

Lake Maggiore is the second-largest lake in Italy and is known for its serene atmosphere, beautiful villas, and the enchanting Borromean Islands. It's less crowded than Lake Como or Lake Garda, making it perfect for those seeking a relaxing escape.

Top Attractions at Lake Maggiore

☐ Isola Bella – A magnificent island featuring the 17th-century Palazzo Borromeo and stunning baroque gardens.

☐ Isola Madre – Famous for its botanical gardens and exotic plants.

🏠 Stresa – A charming lakeside town with luxury hotels and fantastic lakefront promenades.

☐ Mottarone Cable Car – Take a ride up to Mottarone Mountain for breathtaking views of the Alps and the lake.

☐ Visit the Hermitage of Santa Caterina del Sasso – A stunning monastery built into the cliffs overlooking the lake.

💡 Pro Tip: Spring and summer are the best times to visit Lake Maggiore, as the gardens and landscapes are in full bloom.

Best Routes for Scenic Drives and Lakeside Towns

If you want to experience all three lakes in one road trip, follow this perfect scenic itinerary:

🚗 Start in Milan – Rent a car and drive 1 hour north to Lake Como.

🚗 Explore Lake Como – Spend 2-3 days visiting Bellagio, Varenna, and Tremezzo.

🚗 Head to Lake Garda – Drive 2.5 hours to Sirmione and spend 2-3 days exploring Malcesine, Limone, and nearby attractions.

🚗 Drive to Lake Maggiore – Take a 2-hour scenic drive to Stresa and the Borromean Islands. Spend 1-2 days relaxing before heading back to Milan.

💡 Alternative Option: If you don't want to drive long distances, you can take advantage of ferries and trains that connect many of these lakeside towns.

The Milan to Venice Cultural Drive

Exploring Historic Cities Like Verona, Bergamo, and Padua

A road trip from Milan to Venice is not just about the destination—it's about the incredible historical cities, rich culture, and stunning landscapes along the way. This cultural drive takes you through some of Italy's most iconic cities, where medieval charm, Renaissance art, and centuries-old traditions come to life.

Starting in Milan, the fashion and financial capital of Italy, this journey will take you through the romantic city of Verona, the medieval beauty of Bergamo, and the artistic treasures of Padua, before ending in the breathtaking canal city of Venice.

This scenic and culture-filled route is perfect for history buffs, architecture lovers, and those who want to explore Italy's artistic heritage at their own pace.

Stop 1: Milan – The Stylish Gateway to Northern Italy

📍 Starting Point: Milan

☐ Best for: Fashion, history, and Renaissance art

Milan, Italy's fashion capital, is more than just high-end shopping and designer boutiques. It's a city of art, history, and stunning architecture.

Top Attractions in Milan

🏰 Duomo di Milano – The largest and most intricate Gothic cathedral in Italy. Don't miss the panoramic rooftop views!

🎭 Teatro alla Scala – One of the most famous opera houses in the world, hosting legendary performances.

☐ The Last Supper – Leonardo da Vinci's masterpiece, housed at Santa Maria delle Grazie.

☐ Sforza Castle – A 15th-century fortress filled with museums and art galleries.

☐ Galleria Vittorio Emanuele II – A luxurious 19th-century shopping gallery with high-end boutiques and historic cafés.

💡 Pro Tip: If you're short on time, a half-day in Milan is enough to explore its most iconic sites before hitting the road.

Stop 2: Bergamo – A Hidden Medieval Gem

📍 Distance from Milan: 58 km (1-hour drive)

☐ Best for: Medieval architecture, cobbled streets, panoramic views

Often overlooked by travelers, Bergamo is one of Italy's most charming cities, divided into two parts:

🏰 Città Alta (Upper Town) – A beautifully preserved medieval old town, accessible by a funicular railway.

☐ Città Bassa (Lower Town) – The modern part of the city with vibrant piazzas and restaurants.

Top Attractions in Bergamo

🏰 Piazza Vecchia – A stunning medieval square, surrounded by elegant Renaissance buildings.

⛪ Basilica di Santa Maria Maggiore – A breathtaking Romanesque church with elaborate frescoes and a golden ceiling.

🚶‍♂️ Walk the Venetian Walls – A UNESCO World Heritage Site offering spectacular views over the city.

☐ Funicular Ride – Take a scenic funicular up to Città Alta for an unforgettable experience.

💡 Pro Tip: Spend half a day in Bergamo before continuing your journey towards Verona.

Stop 3: Verona – The City of Love and Shakespeare

📍 Distance from Bergamo: 117 km (1.5-hour drive)

☐ Best for: Romance, Shakespearean history, and Roman architecture

Verona is one of Italy's most romantic cities, famously known as the setting for Shakespeare's Romeo and Juliet. But beyond the Shakespearean legend, Verona is a city filled with Roman ruins, medieval castles, and charming piazzas.

Top Attractions in Verona

☐ Piazza delle Erbe – The heart of Verona, surrounded by colorful Renaissance buildings and lively cafés.

🎭 Arena di Verona – A 2,000-year-old Roman amphitheater, still hosting world-class opera performances.

💕 Juliet's House (Casa di Giulietta) – A popular attraction where visitors can see Juliet's famous balcony and leave love notes on the walls.

🏰 Castelvecchio – A medieval fortress and museum, offering stunning views over the Adige River.

🌉 Ponte Pietra – A Roman bridge that provides a perfect photo opportunity.

💡 Pro Tip: Sunset in Verona is magical—head to Castel San Pietro for an unforgettable panoramic view over the city.

Stop 4: Padua – The City of Science and Faith

📍 Distance from Verona: 88 km (1-hour drive)

☐ Best for: Renaissance art, religious history, and botanical gardens

Padua (Padova) is one of Italy's oldest university cities and is home to some of the most stunning frescoes and churches in the country. It's a hidden treasure that blends academic prestige, religious significance, and artistic masterpieces.

Top Attractions in Padua

🎨 Scrovegni Chapel – Home to Giotto's breathtaking frescoes, considered one of the greatest masterpieces of Western art.

⛪ Basilica of Saint Anthony of Padua – A stunning pilgrimage site, dedicated to the city's patron saint.

☐ Prato della Valle – One of Europe's largest squares, surrounded by statues and beautiful fountains.

🌿 Orto Botanico di Padova – The world's first botanical garden, established in 1545.

💡 Pro Tip: If you're a lover of art and history, consider spending a full day in Padua before heading to Venice.

Stop 5: Venice – The Grand Finale

📍 Distance from Padua: 41 km (45-minute drive)

☐ Best for: Canals, gondola rides, and historical landmarks

Finally, your journey ends in Venice, one of the most unique and romantic cities in the world. With its winding canals, historic palaces, and world-famous art, Venice is a masterpiece.

Top Attractions in Venice

🛥 Grand Canal & Gondola Ride – Experience the city from the water with a classic Venetian gondola ride.

🏰 Piazza San Marco (St. Mark's Square) – The iconic heart of Venice, home to St. Mark's Basilica and the Doge's Palace.

☐ Doge's Palace – A masterpiece of Venetian Gothic architecture, filled with art and history.

🌉 Rialto Bridge – One of the most famous bridges in Venice, perfect for photos and shopping.

☐ Murano & Burano – Take a boat trip to Murano (famous for glassmaking) and Burano (famous for its colorful houses and lace production).

💡 Pro Tip: Venice is best explored on foot or by vaporetto (water bus). Cars are not allowed in the city, so park your vehicle at Piazzale Roma before venturing into the canals.

Best Route and Driving Tips

🚗 Day 1: Milan → Bergamo (1-hour drive) → Spend half a day exploring Bergamo.

🚗 Day 2: Bergamo → Verona (1.5-hour drive) → Spend a full day in Verona.

🚗 Day 3: Verona → Padua (1-hour drive) → Spend a full day exploring Padua.

🚗 Day 4: Padua → Venice (45-minute drive) → Park at Piazzale Roma and explore Venice.

This 4 to 5-day itinerary offers the best balance of cultural exploration, scenic beauty, and historical immersion along one of Italy's most iconic driving routes.

Must-Visit UNESCO Sites Along the Milan to Venice Cultural Drive

A road trip through Northern Italy is not just about beautiful landscapes and charming towns—it's a journey through history, where some of the world's most remarkable UNESCO World Heritage Sites await. From ancient Roman arenas to Renaissance masterpieces, these UNESCO-listed landmarks add cultural depth to your drive, making every stop more enriching.

Here are the must-visit UNESCO sites along the way, with tips on how to include them in your itinerary.

1. The Last Supper (Milan) – A Renaissance Masterpiece

📍 Location: Santa Maria delle Grazie, Milan

☐ Best Time to Visit: Morning (tickets sell out quickly, so book in advance!)

☐ Entry: Reservation required

One of the most famous paintings in the world, Leonardo da Vinci's The Last Supper, is housed in the Santa Maria delle Grazie monastery. This Renaissance masterpiece, painted between 1495-1498, is a must-see for art lovers and history enthusiasts alike.

💡 Pro Tip: Book your tickets at least two months in advance, as entry slots are limited to preserve the fragile painting.

2. The Venetian Walls of Bergamo – A Medieval Marvel

📍 Location: Città Alta, Bergamo

☐ Best Time to Visit: Sunset for breathtaking panoramic views

☐ Entry: Free

Bergamo's Venetian Walls, built in the 16th century by the Republic of Venice, are a UNESCO World Heritage Site that offer spectacular views over Lombardy. These massive fortifications were designed to protect the city from invaders, but today, they provide one of the most picturesque walks in Italy.

💡 Pro Tip: Take a leisurely stroll along the walls at sunset for stunning golden-hour photography.

3. Verona's Historic Center – The City of Romeo & Juliet

📍 Location: Verona

☐ Best Time to Visit: Early morning (to avoid crowds)

☐ Entry: Free for city exploration, but some landmarks have entrance fees

The entire historic center of Verona is a UNESCO World Heritage Site, and it's easy to see why. The city is home to:

☐ The Arena di Verona – A 2,000-year-old Roman amphitheater, still hosting concerts and opera performances.

💘 Juliet's House (Casa di Giulietta) – Inspired by Shakespeare's Romeo and Juliet, this spot draws thousands of visitors.

🌉 Ponte Pietra – A stunning Roman bridge, perfect for an evening stroll.

💡 Pro Tip: If you love history, take a guided walking tour to uncover Verona's hidden secrets and Roman heritage.

4. Padua's Scrovegni Chapel – A Hidden Artistic Gem

📍 Location: Padua

☐ Best Time to Visit: Early morning (limited visitor slots)

☐ Entry: Advance booking required

The Scrovegni Chapel is home to one of the most important fresco cycles in Western art, painted by Giotto in 1305. This masterpiece of medieval art paved the way for the Renaissance and remains one of Italy's greatest treasures.

💡 Pro Tip: Entry is strictly timed to protect the frescoes, so book your visit in advance and arrive early.

5. Venice's Historic Center & Lagoon – A Floating Masterpiece

📍 Location: Venice

☐ Best Time to Visit: Late afternoon (for magical lighting on the canals)

☐ Entry: Free, but major landmarks like St. Mark's Basilica have fees

Venice is a UNESCO-listed wonder unlike any other city in the world. With its floating palaces, romantic canals, and historic architecture, it's the grand finale of your road trip.

Top UNESCO highlights in Venice:

🏰 St. Mark's Basilica – A breathtaking Byzantine cathedral filled with golden mosaics.

🎭 Doge's Palace – A Gothic masterpiece that was once the heart of Venetian power.

🌉 Rialto Bridge – One of the most iconic bridges in Venice, connecting the Grand Canal.

☐ Murano & Burano – Glassmaking and lace artistry, recognized as part of Venice's intangible heritage.

💡 Pro Tip: Visit St. Mark's Square at sunrise for a crowd-free experience and stunning reflections on the canals.

Best Routes for Wine Lovers: Franciacorta & Prosecco Wine Road

Italy's northern regions are not only famous for art and history—they also produce some of the finest wines in the world. If you love wine tasting and scenic vineyard drives, consider adding one (or both!) of these iconic wine routes to your road trip.

1. Franciacorta Wine Road – Italy's Sparkling Wine Paradise

🍷 Famous for: Italy's finest sparkling wine (Franciacorta DOCG)

📍 Location: Brescia province (between Milan and Verona)

☐ Best Time to Visit: September–October (grape harvest season)

Franciacorta is Italy's answer to Champagne, producing luxurious sparkling wines made with the same traditional method. This stunning wine region, located between Milan and Verona, offers rolling vineyards, charming wineries, and exclusive wine-tasting experiences.

Must-Visit Wineries in Franciacorta

🍇 Ca' del Bosco – One of the most prestigious Franciacorta producers.

🍇 Bellavista – Famous for elegant, long-aged sparkling wines.

🍇 Berlucchi – The birthplace of Franciacorta DOCG, offering historic cellars and tastings.

💡 Pro Tip: Stay overnight at a countryside wine resort to experience Franciacorta's relaxing atmosphere.

2. Prosecco Wine Road – The Land of Bubbles

🍷 Famous for: Prosecco DOCG (Italy's most popular sparkling wine)

📍 Location: Conegliano-Valdobbiadene, Veneto

☐ Best Time to Visit: Spring (blooming vineyards) or Fall (grape harvest)

For lovers of lighter, refreshing bubbles, the Prosecco Wine Road in the Veneto region is a must-visit. This scenic route stretches between Conegliano and Valdobbiadene, offering breathtaking vineyard landscapes and charming hilltop villages.

Must-Visit Wineries on the Prosecco Route

☐ Villa Sandi – A historic winery with elegant tastings.

☐ Nino Franco – One of the oldest Prosecco producers, known for its refined flavors.

☐ Bisol – Specializing in high-end Prosecco Superiore DOCG.

💡 Pro Tip: Take a Prosecco picnic in the vineyards—many wineries offer private tasting experiences with local cheeses and meats.

CHAPTER FOUR

The Tuscany and Chianti Wine Route: A Journey Through Italy's Heartland

Central Italy is a dream destination for road trippers, and no region captures the essence of la dolce vita quite like Tuscany. From the renaissance beauty of Florence to the medieval charm of Siena, and the vine-covered hills of Chianti, this route is the ultimate Italian road trip for lovers of history, art, and wine.

With every turn of the road, you'll find rolling golden landscapes, centuries-old vineyards, charming stone villages, and world-class cuisine. This Tuscany and Chianti Wine Route takes you through some of the most iconic destinations in Italy's heartland, making it an unforgettable journey filled with breathtaking scenery, cultural treasures, and gastronomic delights.

So, let's hit the road and explore the best of Tuscany and Chianti!

🚗 The Best Route for Your Tuscany & Chianti Road Trip

Starting Point: Florence – The Cradle of the Renaissance

📍 Must-Visit Attractions:

✓☐ Piazza del Duomo – Marvel at the iconic Cathedral of Santa Maria del Fiore, Giotto's Bell Tower, and the Baptistery.

✓☐ Uffizi Gallery – Home to world-famous paintings by Botticelli, Michelangelo, and Leonardo da Vinci.

✓☐ Ponte Vecchio – The oldest bridge in Florence, lined with charming jewelry shops.

✓☐ Piazzale Michelangelo – The best panoramic view of Florence, especially at sunset.

💡 Pro Tip: Spend at least two days in Florence to fully enjoy its art, history, and vibrant atmosphere before heading into the Tuscan countryside.

Stop 1: Greve in Chianti – Gateway to Wine Country

📍 Distance from Florence: 30 km (45 min drive)

Greve in Chianti is the heart of Chianti Classico wine country, known for its rustic charm and wine heritage. This picturesque town is home to historic wineries and a lively town square, making it a great place to begin your Tuscan wine adventure.

🍷 Top Experiences in Greve in Chianti:

✓☐ Visit the Wine Museum – A fascinating look at the history of Chianti winemaking.

✓☐ Wine tasting at Castello di Verrazzano – One of the most famous wineries in Chianti.

✓☐ Explore Piazza Matteotti – The charming main square with traditional cafés and shops.

💡 Pro Tip: Buy a Chianti Wine Tasting Card at the local Enoteca Falorni and sample over 100 different wines from the region!

Stop 2: Radda in Chianti – A Medieval Wine Haven

📍 Distance from Greve in Chianti: 20 km (30 min drive)

A fairy-tale hilltop town, Radda in Chianti is a perfect place to soak in medieval charm while sipping some of the best Chianti wines.

🏰 Top Things to Do in Radda in Chianti:

✓☐ Tour the 12th-century walls that surround this charming village.

✓☐ Visit Castello di Volpaia, a historic winery set in a medieval castle.

✓☐ Relax at a countryside vineyard with a farm-to-table lunch.

💡 Pro Tip: Stay overnight at a vineyard agriturismo (farmhouse stay) to experience the authentic Tuscan countryside lifestyle.

Stop 3: Castellina in Chianti – Wine Tasting & Etruscan History

📍 Distance from Radda in Chianti: 15 km (20 min drive)

A mix of history and winemaking, Castellina in Chianti offers Etruscan ruins, medieval streets, and world-class wineries.

🏰 Must-See Attractions in Castellina in Chianti:

✓☐ Explore the Via delle Volte, an ancient underground passage with breathtaking views.

✓☐ Visit the Archaeological Museum of Chianti to learn about the region's Etruscan roots.

✓☐ Taste wines at Rocca delle Macìe, one of Chianti's most famous wineries.

💡 Pro Tip: If you're a history buff, visit the nearby Etruscan Tomb of Montecalvario, an ancient burial site dating back over 2,500 years.

Stop 4: Siena – A Medieval Masterpiece

📍 Distance from Castellina in Chianti: 25 km (35 min drive)

One of Italy's most stunning medieval cities, Siena is famous for its breathtaking architecture, rich history, and world-renowned Palio horse race.

🏰 Must-See Attractions in Siena:

✓☐ Piazza del Campo – One of Europe's most beautiful squares and home to the Palio horse race.

✓☐ Siena Cathedral (Duomo di Siena) – A gothic masterpiece with intricate marble designs.

✓☐ Climb the Torre del Mangia – For panoramic views of Siena's red rooftops and rolling hills.

✓☐ Taste the local dish, Pici Pasta, a hand-rolled thick spaghetti unique to Siena.

💡 Pro Tip: Stay overnight in Siena's historic center to experience the city's magical atmosphere after sunset.

Stop 5: San Gimignano – Tuscany's "Medieval Manhattan"

📍 Distance from Siena: 45 km (1-hour drive)

San Gimignano is famous for its 14 medieval towers, giving it the nickname "the Manhattan of the Middle Ages". This UNESCO-listed town is a must-visit for its stunning architecture, delicious local wine (Vernaccia di San Gimignano), and breathtaking views.

🏰 Must-See Attractions in San Gimignano:

✓☐ Climb Torre Grossa, the tallest medieval tower in town.

✓☐ Try award-winning gelato at Gelateria Dondoli.

✓☐ Sip Vernaccia wine, the region's famous white wine.

💡 Pro Tip: Visit early morning or late afternoon to avoid tourist crowds.

Final Stop: Val d'Orcia – The Most Iconic Tuscan Landscape

📍 Distance from San Gimignano: 80 km (1.5-hour drive)

If you've ever seen a postcard of Tuscany's rolling green hills dotted with cypress trees, it was likely taken in Val d'Orcia. This UNESCO World Heritage landscape is the perfect place to end your Tuscany road trip.

⛰ Must-See Villages in Val d'Orcia:

✅ Pienza – The birthplace of Pecorino cheese, with stunning panoramic views.

✅ Montepulciano – Famous for Vino Nobile di Montepulciano, a robust red wine.

✅ Montalcino – Home to Brunello di Montalcino, one of Italy's most prestigious wines.

💡 Pro Tip: Drive the SR2 road from San Quirico d'Orcia to Pienza for the most breathtaking Tuscan views.

The Rome to Florence Historic Highway: A Journey Through Italy's Timeless Beauty

Traveling from Rome to Florence is more than just a drive—it's an immersive journey through the heart of Italy, filled with history, culture, and breathtaking landscapes. This legendary route, stretching approximately 300 km (186 miles), is one of the most scenic and historically rich road trips in the country. Along the way, you'll discover ancient ruins, medieval hilltop towns, Renaissance masterpieces, and world-famous vineyards, making it a must-do for travelers seeking an authentic Italian experience.

With each stop, you'll feel as if you're stepping back in time, from the Roman Empire's grandeur to the artistic brilliance of the Renaissance. Buckle up and get ready for a road trip filled with hidden gems, UNESCO-listed sites, and unforgettable landscapes as we explore the Rome to Florence Historic Highway.

🚗 The Best Route for Your Rome to Florence Road Trip

While the A1 Autostrada (Autostrada del Sole) is the fastest way to travel from Rome to Florence, this road trip takes a scenic detour through the winding roads of Tuscany and Umbria, where you'll encounter some of the most beautiful towns and landscapes in Italy.

□ Stop 1: Rome – The Eternal City (Starting Point)

📍 Starting Point: Rome, Italy

No Italian road trip would be complete without exploring the wonders of Rome before setting off. If you haven't already, take some time to visit:

✓□ The Colosseum – Walk in the footsteps of gladiators in this ancient arena.

✓☐ The Vatican City – Marvel at The Vatican Museums, the Sistine Chapel, and St. Peter's Basilica.

✓☐ The Pantheon – One of the best-preserved monuments from Ancient Rome.

✓☐ Trevi Fountain – Toss a coin and make a wish before embarking on your journey!

💡 Pro Tip: Rent your car after exploring Rome to avoid navigating the city's busy traffic and ZTL (restricted traffic zones).

🏰 Stop 2: Civita di Bagnoregio – The "Dying Town"

📍 Distance from Rome: 120 km (1.5-hour drive)

Known as "La città che muore" (The Dying Town), Civita di Bagnoregio is an enchanting medieval village perched atop a hill, slowly being eroded by the elements.

☐ Top Things to See & Do in Civita di Bagnoregio:

✓☐ Walk across the pedestrian bridge to the town—it's the only way to access it!

✓☐ Stroll through the charming medieval streets, where time seems to stand still.

✓☐ Enjoy panoramic views of the surrounding valleys and canyons.

💡 Pro Tip: Visit in the early morning or late afternoon for fewer crowds and the best golden-hour views.

🏠 Stop 3: Orvieto – A Hilltop Wonder in Umbria

📍 Distance from Civita di Bagnoregio: 24 km (30-minute drive)

Orvieto is one of Italy's best-kept secrets, known for its stunning Gothic cathedral, underground caves, and world-class white wine.

🏰 Top Attractions in Orvieto:

✓☐ Orvieto Cathedral (Duomo di Orvieto) – A Gothic masterpiece with dazzling frescoes.

✓☐ St. Patrick's Well (Pozzo di San Patrizio) – A spiral well built in the 16th century.

✓☐ Orvieto Underground Tour – Explore the network of tunnels and caves beneath the city.

✓☐ Try a glass of Orvieto Classico wine, one of Italy's finest white wines.

💡 Pro Tip: Stay overnight in Orvieto to enjoy its romantic evening atmosphere without the day-tripper crowds.

🍷 Stop 4: Montepulciano – The Jewel of Tuscany

📍 Distance from Orvieto: 80 km (1-hour drive)

Montepulciano is a stunning Renaissance town known for its vineyards and award-winning Vino Nobile di Montepulciano.

🍷 Must-Visit Places in Montepulciano:

✓☐ Piazza Grande – The historic center surrounded by Renaissance palaces.

✓☐ Wine tasting at Cantina Contucci, one of the oldest wineries in Montepulciano.

✓☐ Visit San Biagio Church, a beautiful Tuscan church with breathtaking views.

💡 Pro Tip: If you're a wine lover, this is the perfect place to book a vineyard tour and taste Tuscany's famous reds.

🌻 Stop 5: Pienza – The Home of Pecorino Cheese

📍 Distance from Montepulciano: 15 km (20-minute drive)

A UNESCO-listed town, Pienza is the perfect blend of Renaissance beauty and delicious local flavors.

☐ Best Things to Do in Pienza:

✓☐ Walk along the panoramic walls for breathtaking views of the Val d'Orcia.

✓☐ Try Pecorino di Pienza, a world-famous sheep's milk cheese.

✓☐ Explore Piazza Pio II, a perfectly designed Renaissance square.

💡 Pro Tip: Visit a cheese farm in the countryside to see how Pecorino cheese is made.

◻ Stop 6: San Gimignano – The City of Towers

📍 Distance from Pienza: 100 km (1.5-hour drive)

San Gimignano, often called "Medieval Manhattan," is known for its 14 medieval towers that dominate the skyline.

🏰 Top Attractions in San Gimignano:

✓◻ Climb Torre Grossa for breathtaking views of the Tuscan countryside.

✓◻ Visit the Collegiate Church of San Gimignano, with incredible frescoes.

✓◻ Try the award-winning gelato at Gelateria Dondoli.

💡 Pro Tip: The town is busiest during the day, so arrive early in the morning or stay for sunset to enjoy it without the crowds.

🏁 Final Stop: Florence – The Birthplace of the Renaissance

📍 Distance from San Gimignano: 60 km (1-hour drive)

Your Rome to Florence road trip ends in one of the most beautiful cities in the world. Florence is an open-air museum, where every street and piazza holds a piece of history.

🎨 Must-Visit Attractions in Florence:

✓☐ The Uffizi Gallery – Home to masterpieces by Michelangelo, Botticelli, and Raphael.

✓☐ Ponte Vecchio – The oldest bridge in Florence, lined with historic shops.

✓☐ Climb the Duomo (Cathedral of Santa Maria del Fiore) for unbeatable views of the city.

✓☐ Piazzale Michelangelo – A must-visit for the best sunset views over Florence.

💡 Pro Tip: Florence has a ZTL (restricted traffic zone), so drop off your rental car after arriving and explore the city on foot.

Exploring the Rome to Florence Historic Highway: A Journey Through Time and Beauty

Italy is a country where history, culture, and natural beauty blend seamlessly. Nowhere is this more evident than on the road trip from Rome to Florence, a route that takes travelers through some of Italy's most charming historic cities, ancient Roman roads, and stunning landscapes. As you drive through the heart of central Italy, you'll encounter towns steeped in Etruscan history, medieval charm, and Renaissance grandeur, all while enjoying breathtaking countryside views and hidden gems that lie just beyond the well-trodden tourist paths.

This road trip isn't just about getting from Rome to Florence; it's about immersing yourself in centuries of history, savoring local flavors, and discovering scenic detours that will leave you spellbound. Buckle up and get ready for an unforgettable drive through the soul of Italy!

☐ Stop 1: Orvieto – A Journey into Etruscan and Medieval Italy

📍 Distance from Rome: 120 km (1.5-hour drive)

Orvieto is a hilltop town in Umbria, dramatically perched on a volcanic tuff cliff. With its Etruscan origins, medieval streets, and Renaissance influences, Orvieto is a must-visit destination.

✨ What Makes Orvieto Special?

✓☐ Etruscan Underground City – Beneath Orvieto lies a network of underground caves, tunnels, and wells dating back to Etruscan times. Take a guided tour to explore this hidden world.

✓☐ Orvieto Cathedral (Duomo di Orvieto) – This magnificent Gothic masterpiece is adorned with stunning mosaics and features the famous Chapel of San Brizio, with frescoes by Luca Signorelli that influenced Michelangelo.

✓☐ St. Patrick's Well (Pozzo di San Patrizio) – A remarkable engineering feat from the 16th century, this double-helix well was built to ensure water supply during sieges.

✓☐ Piazza della Repubblica – The perfect spot to soak in the town's historic charm over a cup of espresso.

✓☐ Local Wine Tasting – Orvieto is known for its crisp white wines (Orvieto Classico). Visit a local enoteca (wine bar) for a glass of this refreshing regional favorite.

💡 Pro Tip: If you have extra time, drive to the nearby Lake Bolsena, a stunning Crater Lake perfect for a peaceful picnic or a lakeside lunch.

🛕 Stop 2: Assisi – The Spiritual and Artistic Heart of Italy

📍 Distance from Orvieto: 90 km (1.5-hour drive)

Nestled in the rolling hills of Umbria, Assisi is world-famous as the birthplace of Saint Francis of Assisi, one of Italy's most beloved saints. This town is a UNESCO World Heritage site, filled with religious significance, breathtaking art, and medieval charm.

✨ Top Things to See in Assisi

✓☐ Basilica of St. Francis of Assisi – The crown jewel of the town, this double-layered basilica houses Gio

tto's stunning frescoes depicting the life of St. Francis.

✓☐ Rocca Maggiore – A medieval fortress offering breathtaking panoramic views of the Umbrian countryside.

✓☐ Piazza del Comune – The heart of the town, featuring the Temple of Minerva, a Roman structure that dates back to the 1st century BC.

✓☐ San Damiano Monastery – A peaceful retreat where Saint Francis wrote the famous "Canticle of the Sun".

✓☐ Local Specialties – Try Torta al Testo, a delicious Umbrian flatbread often stuffed with local meats and cheeses.

💡 Pro Tip: Assisi gets crowded with pilgrims, so arrive early in the morning for a peaceful experience at the Basilica.

☐ Stop 3: Arezzo – A Hidden Renaissance Gem

📍 Distance from Assisi: 90 km (1.5-hour drive)

Often overshadowed by Florence and Siena, Arezzo is a hidden Renaissance gem filled with art, history, and one of Italy's best antique markets. It is the birthplace of renowned poet Petrarch and home to some of Piero della Francesca's most famous frescoes.

✨ What to See in Arezzo

✓☐ Piazza Grande – One of the most beautiful medieval squares in Italy, surrounded by elegant Renaissance buildings.

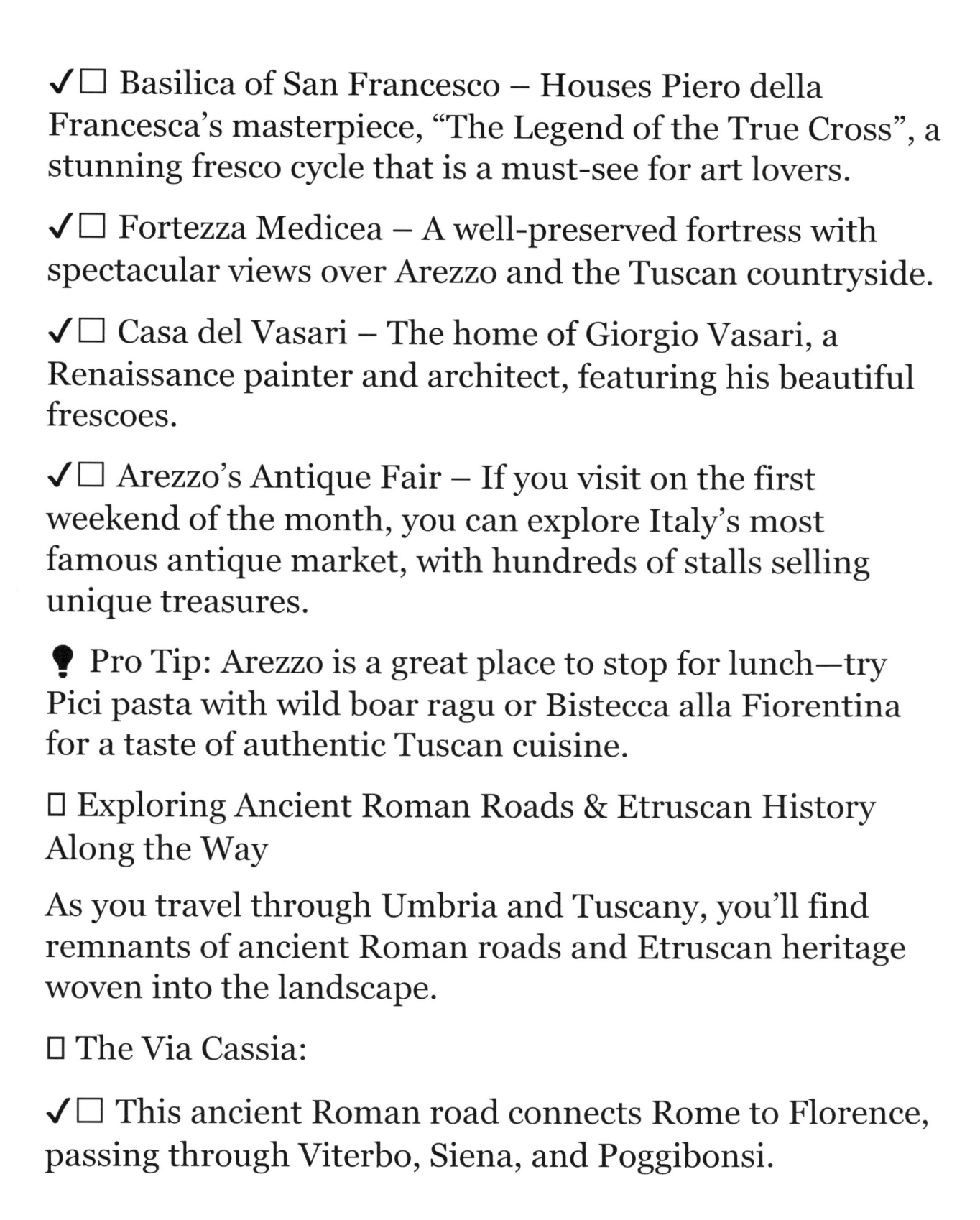

✓☐ Basilica of San Francesco – Houses Piero della Francesca's masterpiece, "The Legend of the True Cross", a stunning fresco cycle that is a must-see for art lovers.

✓☐ Fortezza Medicea – A well-preserved fortress with spectacular views over Arezzo and the Tuscan countryside.

✓☐ Casa del Vasari – The home of Giorgio Vasari, a Renaissance painter and architect, featuring his beautiful frescoes.

✓☐ Arezzo's Antique Fair – If you visit on the first weekend of the month, you can explore Italy's most famous antique market, with hundreds of stalls selling unique treasures.

💡 Pro Tip: Arezzo is a great place to stop for lunch—try Pici pasta with wild boar ragu or Bistecca alla Fiorentina for a taste of authentic Tuscan cuisine.

☐ Exploring Ancient Roman Roads & Etruscan History Along the Way

As you travel through Umbria and Tuscany, you'll find remnants of ancient Roman roads and Etruscan heritage woven into the landscape.

☐ The Via Cassia:

✓☐ This ancient Roman road connects Rome to Florence, passing through Viterbo, Siena, and Poggibonsi.

✓☐ It was one of the main trade routes of the Roman Empire, and sections of the original stone pavement still exist today.

☐ The Etruscan Legacy:

✓☐ Towns like Orvieto, Volterra, and Cortona were once major Etruscan settlements, and you can still visit their ancient tombs, artifacts, and necropolises.

✓☐ Stop at the Etruscan Museum of Chiusi or the Tomb of the Leopards in Tarquinia to uncover this fascinating pre-Roman civilization.

🏞 Scenic Landscapes and Off-the-Beaten-Path Locations

One of the best parts of this road trip is the breathtaking countryside you'll drive through.

✓☐ The Val d'Orcia – This UNESCO-listed valley in Tuscany features rolling hills, cypress-lined roads, and golden wheat fields that look like a Renaissance painting.

✓☐ Crete Senesi – A lunar-like landscape with unique clay hills, just outside Siena.

✓☐ The Umbrian Countryside – A picturesque region filled with olive groves, vineyards, and sunflower fields.

💡 Hidden Gem Alert! Stop in Bagno Vignoni, a charming medieval village known for its hot springs and scenic piazza filled with thermal waters!

The Umbria and Marche Countryside Drive: A Journey Through Italy's Hidden Heart

When people think of Italy, they often picture Tuscany's rolling hills, Rome's historic grandeur, or Venice's romantic canals. But for those who crave a road trip filled with authentic medieval charm, breathtaking countryside, and lesser-known coastal gems, the Umbria and Marche countryside drive is a dream come true.

This journey takes you through Italy's "Green Heart" (Umbria) and into the stunning landscapes of the Marche region, where medieval towns, rolling vineyards, and the sparkling Adriatic coastline create an unforgettable mix of history, culture, and natural beauty. Along the way, you'll explore towns rich in art, history, and culinary delights, making this one of the most rewarding road trips in Italy.

🏰 Stop 1: Perugia – The Cultural and Artistic Capital of Umbria

📍 Distance from Florence: 150 km (2-hour drive)

Perugia, the capital of Umbria, is one of Italy's most underrated cities. Famous for its Etruscan roots, medieval architecture, and vibrant cultural scene, Perugia is a perfect first stop on your journey.

✨ Must-See Attractions in Perugia

✅ Piazza IV Novembre – The heart of Perugia, featuring the Fontana Maggiore, a stunning medieval fountain.

✓☐ Rocca Paolina – A fascinating underground fortress built by Pope Paul III, now a hidden city beneath the streets.

✓☐ National Gallery of Umbria – Home to masterpieces by Perugino, Pinturicchio, and other Renaissance greats.

✓☐ Etruscan Well (Pozzo Etrusco) – A remarkable 2,300-year-old water system dating back to the Etruscans.

✓☐ Eurochocolate Festival (October) – If you visit in autumn, don't miss Perugia's famous chocolate festival, celebrating some of Italy's finest sweet creations.

💡 Foodie Tip: Try Baci Perugina, the legendary chocolate and hazelnut truffles made in Perugia!

🕍 Stop 2: Spoleto – A Medieval Jewel with a Rich Heritage

📍 Distance from Perugia: 65 km (1-hour drive)

Nestled in the Umbrian hills, Spoleto is a picturesque medieval town famous for its historic festival, grand architecture, and ancient Roman past.

✨ Highlights of Spoleto

✓☐ Ponte delle Torri – A stunning medieval aqueduct and bridge, offering spectacular views of the valley.

✓☐ Spoleto Cathedral (Duomo di Spoleto) – Home to frescoes by Filippo Lippi, one of the Renaissance's most celebrated painters.

✓☐ Rocca Albornoziana – A majestic fortress that once guarded the town and now houses a museum.

✓☐ Teatro Romano – A well-preserved ancient Roman amphitheater still used for performances today.

✓☐ Festival dei Due Mondi (June-July) – A world-renowned arts and music festival that transforms Spoleto into a cultural hub.

💡 Hidden Gem Alert! Take a short detour to the Monteluco Forest, a sacred wooded area once home to hermits and monks seeking solitude.

🎨 Stop 3: Urbino – The Renaissance Gem of Italy

📍 Distance from Spoleto: 140 km (2-hour drive)

Urbino is a UNESCO-listed town that feels like stepping into a Renaissance painting. Birthplace of Raphael, one of the most celebrated painters of the era, Urbino is a cultural and architectural masterpiece.

✨ Top Attractions in Urbino

✓☐ Palazzo Ducale – A stunning Renaissance palace and home to the Galleria Nazionale delle Marche, featuring works by Raphael, Piero della Francesca, and Titian.

✓☐ Casa Natale di Raffaello – The birthplace of Raphael, now a museum dedicated to his early life and works.

✓☐ Oratory of St. John the Baptist – Famous for its breathtaking frescoes depicting the life of St. John the Baptist.

✓☐ Fortezza Albornoz – A hilltop fortress with panoramic views of Urbino's rooftops and surrounding countryside.

✓☐ University of Urbino – One of Italy's oldest and most prestigious universities, adding a youthful energy to this historic town.

💡 Scenic Drive Tip: Take the winding road from Urbino to Gola del Furlo, a gorgeous limestone gorge perfect for a quick stop to admire the dramatic landscapes.

🚗 Stop 4: The Adriatic Coast – A Drive Along the Sea

📍 Distance from Urbino: 60 km (1-hour drive to Fano, then along the coast)

After exploring Umbria's medieval wonders and Urbino's Renaissance charm, it's time to hit the coastline and soak in the fresh sea air along the Adriatic Sea. The Marche region's coastline is less crowded than the Amalfi Coast but equally stunning, with golden beaches, charming fishing villages, and scenic coastal roads.

✨ Best Stops Along the Adriatic Drive

✓☐ Fano – A coastal town with Roman ruins, sandy beaches, and excellent seafood restaurants.

✓☐ Senigallia – Famous for its soft, golden beaches and the Rotonda a Mare, an elegant Art Nouveau structure by the sea.

✓☐ Conero Riviera – One of Italy's best-kept secrets, featuring crystal-clear waters, limestone cliffs, and secluded beaches like Spiaggia delle Due Sorelle.

✓☐ San Benedetto del Tronto – A lively beach town with a beautiful palm-lined promenade, perfect for a seaside stroll.

💡 Pro Tip: If you love seafood, try Brodetto, a traditional Marche fish stew, served with crusty bread!

🍽 Best Local Food Experiences Along the Way

Every stop on this journey offers unforgettable culinary delights. Here are some must-try dishes:

☐ Umbria:

✓☐ Truffle Pasta (Strangozzi al Tartufo) – Umbria is known as Italy's truffle capital, and this simple but flavorful pasta dish is a must.

✓☐ Porchetta – A savory, herb-roasted pork dish, perfect for a roadside picnic.

🍷 Marche:

✓☐ Olive all'Ascolana – Deep-fried stuffed olives filled with meat, a regional specialty.

✓☐ Verdicchio Wine – A crisp white wine, perfect for pairing with seafood.

🏁 Final Thoughts: A Hidden Gem Road Trip Through Italy

This Umbria and Marche countryside drive is a true hidden gem of an Italian road trip. It offers the perfect blend of history, nature, and coastal beauty, without the overwhelming crowds of more famous routes.

✓☐ History lovers will enjoy the ancient Etruscan and medieval sites.

✓☐ Food enthusiasts will savor the local truffles, seafood, and wines.

✓☐ Scenic explorers will marvel at the rolling countryside, hilltop villages, and coastal drives.

Greve in Chianti

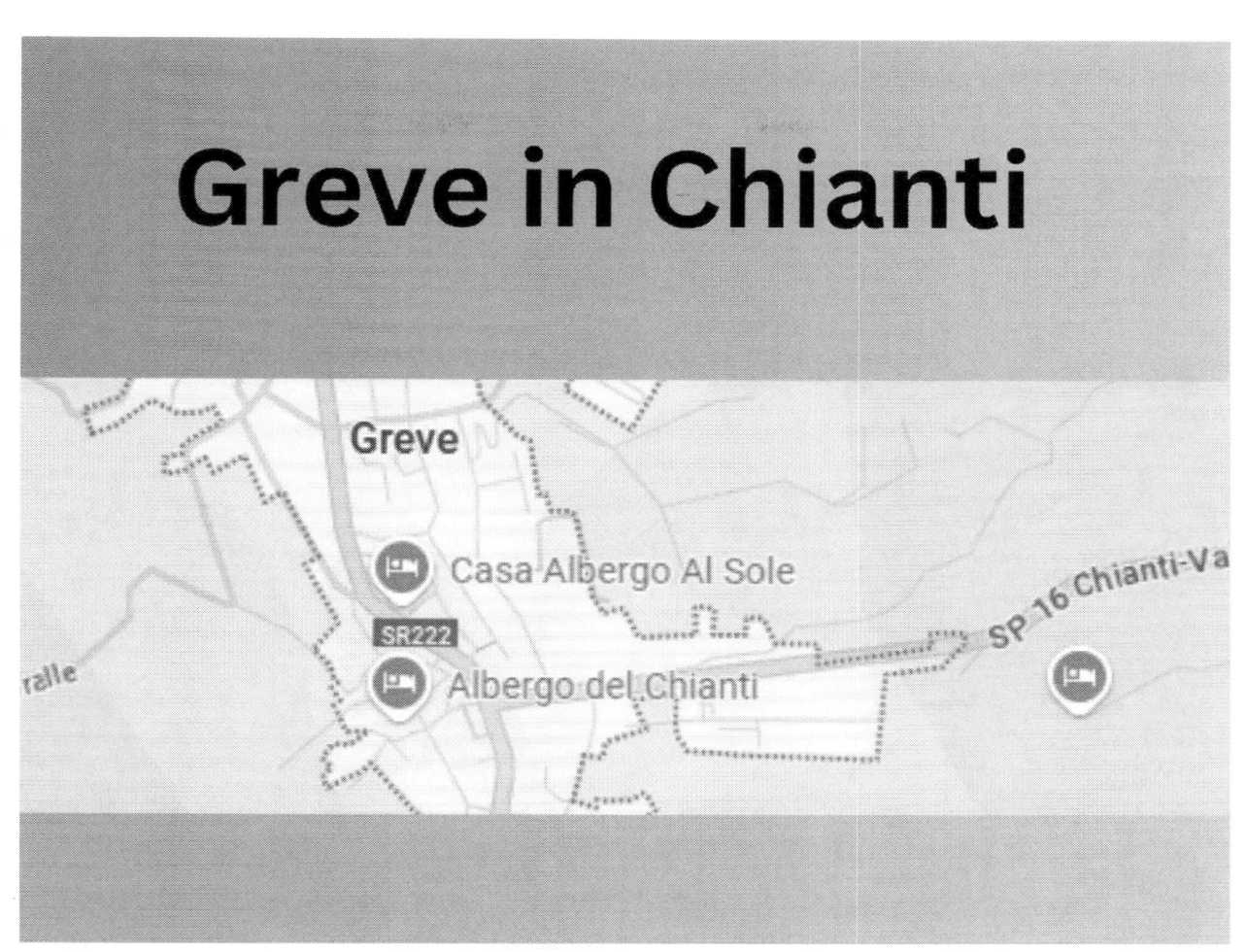

SCAN HERE

HOW TO USE QR CODE
- Open your phone's camera app or download scanner app from play store or app store
- point the camera at the QR code for a few seconds (no need to take a phone)
- A link should appear on the display leading you the location of the code

Radda in Chianti

SCAN HERE

HOW TO USE QR CODE
- Open your phone's camera app or download scanner app from play store or app store
- point the camera at the QR code for a few seconds (no need to take a phone)
- A link should appear on the display leading you the location of the code

Castellina in Chianti

SCAN HERE

HOW TO USE QR CODE
- Open your phone's camera app or download scanner app from play store or app store
- point the camera at the QR code for a few seconds (no need to take a phone)
- A link should appear on the display leading you the location of the code

Siena

SCAN HERE

HOW TO USE QR CODE
- Open your phone's camera app or download scanner app from play store or app store
- point the camera at the QR code for a few seconds (no need to take a phone)
- A link should appear on the display leading you the location of the code

Rome

SCAN HERE

HOW TO USE QR CODE
- Open your phone's camera app or download scanner app from play store or app store
- point the camera at the QR code for a few seconds (no need to take a phone)
- A link should appear on the display leading you the location of the code

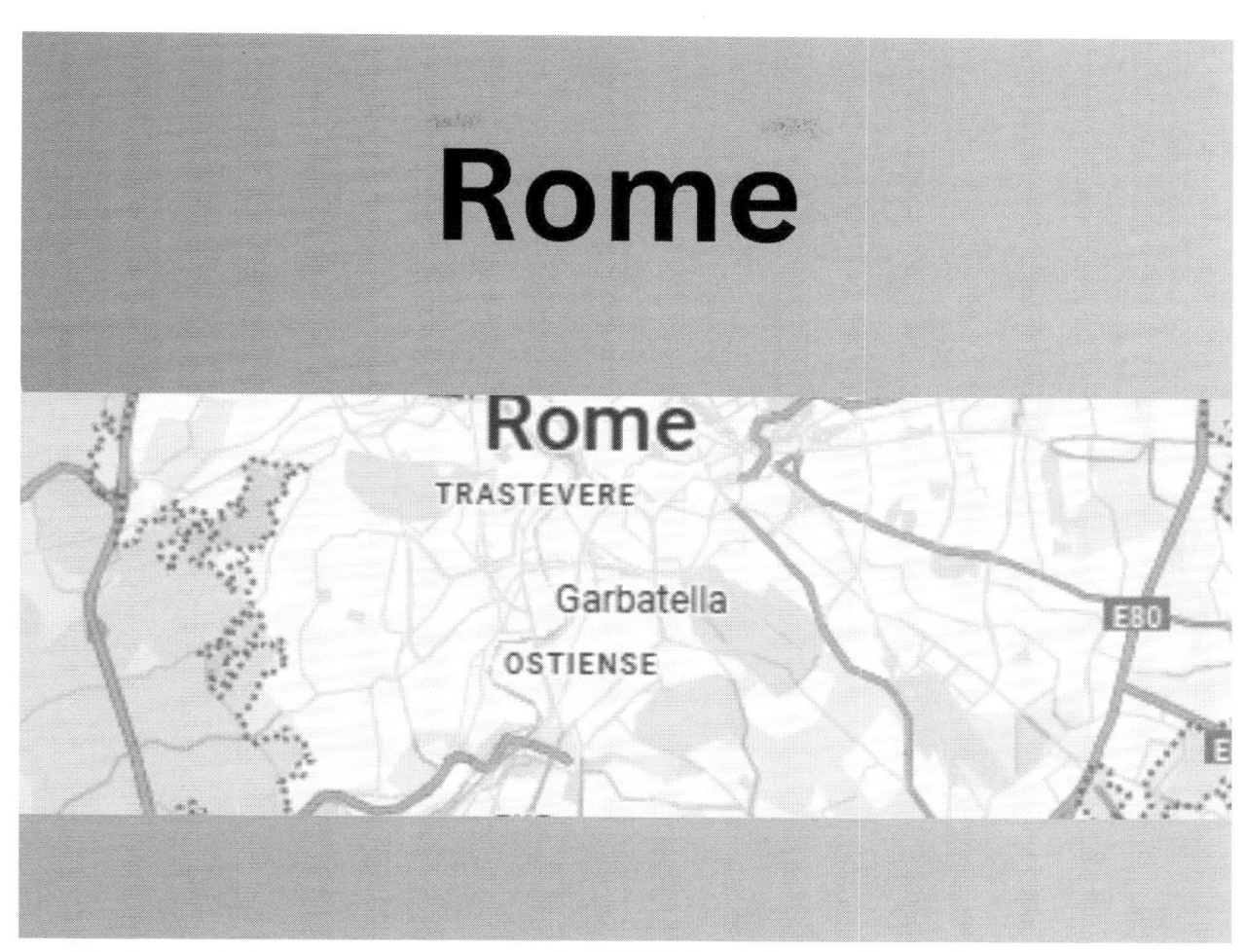

Civita di Bagnoregio

SCAN HERE

HOW TO USE QR CODE
- Open your phone's camera app or download scanner app from play store or app store
- point the camera at the QR code for a few seconds (no need to take a phone)
- A link should appear on the display leading you the location of the code

Orvieto

SCAN HERE

HOW TO USE QR CODE
- Open your phone's camera app or download scanner app from play store or app store
- point the camera at the QR code for a few seconds (no need to take a phone)
- A link should appear on the display leading you the location of the code

Pienza

SCAN HERE

HOW TO USE QR CODE
- Open your phone's camera app or download scanner app from play store or app store
- point the camera at the QR code for a few seconds (no need to take a phone)
- A link should appear on the display leading you the location of the code

Florence

SCAN HERE

HOW TO USE QR CODE
- Open your phone's camera app or download scanner app from play store or app store
- point the camera at the QR code for a few seconds (no need to take a phone)
- A link should appear on the display leading you the location of the code

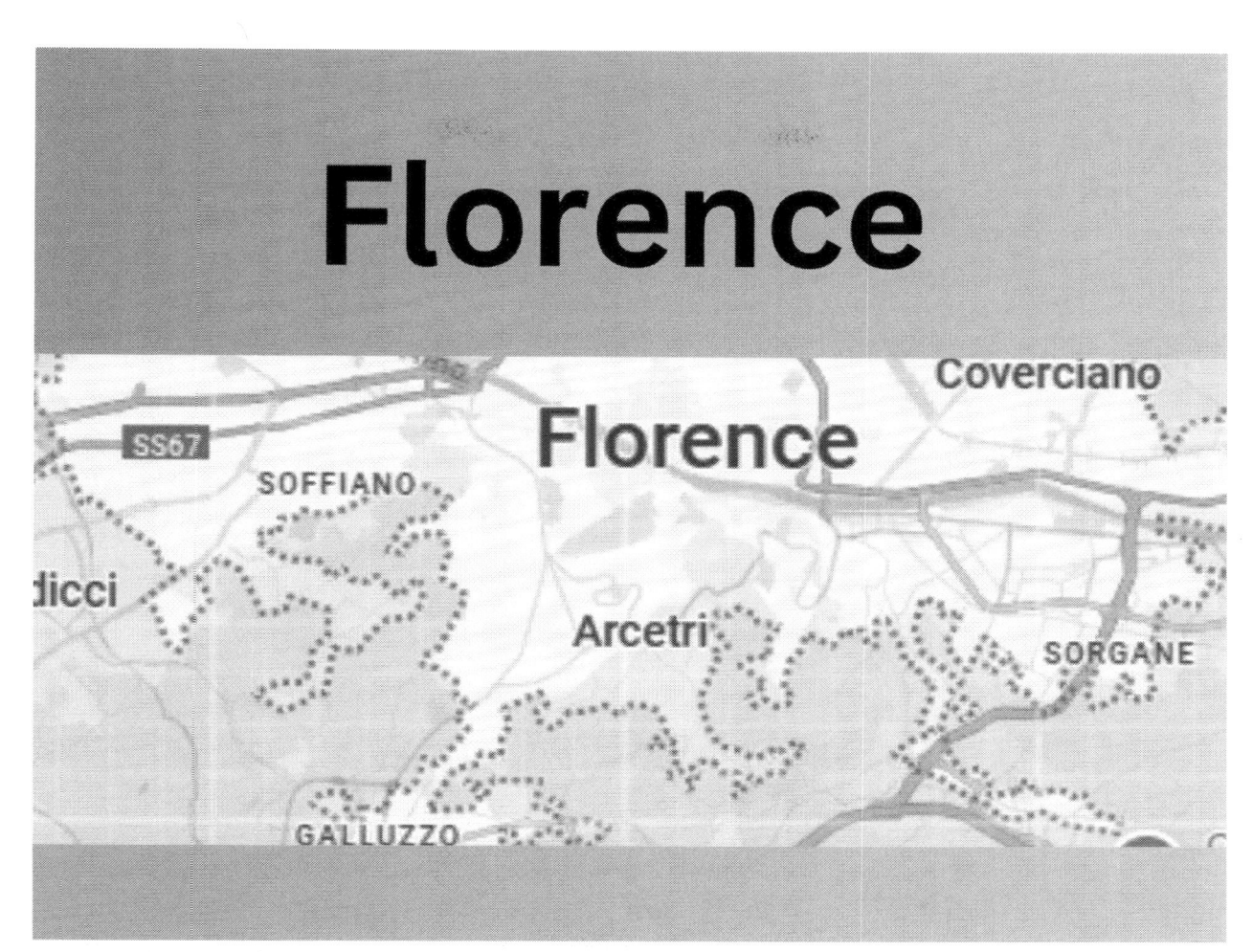

Arezzo

SCAN HERE

HOW TO USE QR CODE
- Open your phone's camera app or download scanner app from play store or app store
- point the camera at the QR code for a few seconds (no need to take a phone)
- A link should appear on the display leading you the location of the code

Assisi

SCAN HERE

HOW TO USE QR CODE
- Open your phone's camera app or download scanner app from play store or app store
- point the camera at the QR code for a few seconds (no need to take a phone)
- A link should appear on the display leading you the location of the code

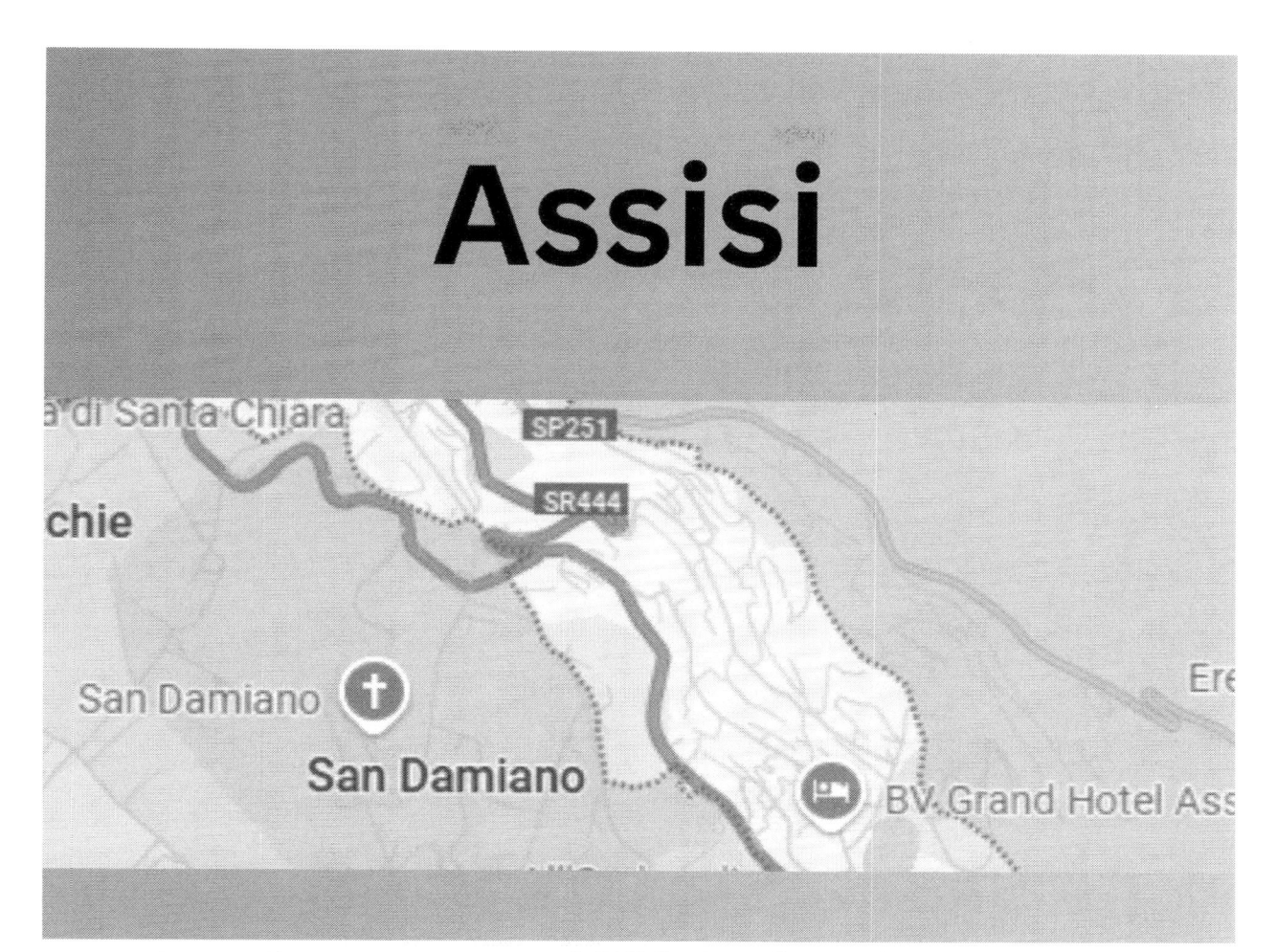

Perugia

SCAN HERE

HOW TO USE QR CODE
- Open your phone's camera app or download scanner app from play store or app store
- point the camera at the QR code for a few seconds (no need to take a phone)
- A link should appear on the display leading you the location of the code

Spoleto

Map showing Croceferro, San Sabino, and Madonna di Lugo

SCAN HERE

HOW TO USE QR CODE
- Open your phone's camera app or download scanner app from play store or app store
- point the camera at the QR code for a few seconds (no need to take a phone)
- A link should appear on the display leading you the location of the code

Umbria

SCAN HERE

HOW TO USE QR CODE
- Open your phone's camera app or download scanner app from play store or app store
- point the camera at the QR code for a few seconds (no need to take a phone)
- A link should appear on the display leading you the location of the code

CHAPTER FIVE

The Amalfi Coast and Naples Drive: A Road Trip Through Italy's Most Breathtaking Coastline

Few road trips in the world can rival the sheer beauty, charm, and cultural richness of the Amalfi Coast and Naples Drive. This route takes you along rugged cliffs, sun-drenched seaside villages, and winding coastal roads, offering a journey through history, cuisine, and some of Italy's most stunning landscapes.

Whether you're chasing scenic views, indulging in authentic Italian flavors, or immersing yourself in centuries of history, this drive is an unforgettable adventure. Buckle up and get ready to explore Naples, the Amalfi Coast, and everything in between!

🚗 Stop 1: Naples – The Gateway to Southern Italy

📍 Starting Point: Naples

Your adventure begins in Naples, a city bursting with energy, history, and the best pizza in the world. Before hitting the road, take time to explore the cultural treasures, lively streets, and mouthwatering cuisine of Italy's third-largest city.

✨ Must-See Attractions in Naples

✓☐ Piazza del Plebiscito – Naples' grand main square, home to the stunning Royal Palace of Naples.

✓☐ Spaccanapoli – The city's historic heart, where narrow streets, bustling markets, and centuries-old churches tell the story of Naples.

✓☐ Castel dell'Ovo – A seaside fortress with breathtaking views of the Bay of Naples.

✓☐ Naples Underground (Napoli Sotterranea) – Explore the hidden tunnels, ancient aqueducts, and WWII bomb shelters beneath the city.

✓☐ National Archaeological Museum – Home to artifacts from Pompeii and Herculaneum, including famous frescoes and mosaics.

💡 Foodie Must-Try: Pizza Margherita – The birthplace of pizza, Naples serves it best with tomato, mozzarella, basil, and a perfectly crisp crust.

🌋 Stop 2: Pompeii & Mount Vesuvius – A Walk Through Ancient History

📍 Distance from Naples: 25 km (30-minute drive)

No trip through Southern Italy is complete without visiting Pompeii, the ancient Roman city frozen in time by Mount Vesuvius' eruption in 79 AD. Walking through its well-preserved streets is a surreal experience, offering a window into life nearly 2,000 years ago.

✨ Top Highlights in Pompeii

✓☐ The Forum – The political and social center of ancient Pompeii.

✓☐ The Amphitheater – One of the oldest surviving Roman arenas, built in 80 BC.

✓☐ The Villa of the Mysteries – Famous for its vivid frescoes depicting ancient rituals.

✓☐ The Lupanar (Ancient Brothel) – A fascinating look at Pompeii's more hidden history.

💡 Adventure Tip: If you're feeling adventurous, take a detour to Mount Vesuvius, where you can hike to the crater for panoramic views of the Bay of Naples.

🌊 Stop 3: Sorrento – The Perfect Amalfi Coast Gateway

📍 Distance from Pompeii: 27 km (40-minute drive)

Perched on dramatic cliffs overlooking the sea, Sorrento is the ideal starting point for exploring the Amalfi Coast. Known for its charming streets, breathtaking views, and delicious limoncello, Sorrento offers the perfect balance between relaxation and adventure.

✨ Things to Do in Sorrento

✓☐ Piazza Tasso – The lively main square, filled with cafés, shops, and restaurants.

✓☐ Marina Grande – A picturesque fishing harbor with colorful boats and seafood restaurants.

✓☐ Villa Comunale Park – Offers one of the best panoramic views over the Bay of Naples.

✓☐ Limoncello Tastings – Try Sorrento's famous lemon liqueur, made from locally grown lemons.

✓☐ Boat to Capri – Consider taking a short ferry ride to the stunning island of Capri, home to the Blue Grotto and luxurious villas.

💡 Scenic Drive Alert: From Sorrento, you officially begin the famous Amalfi Drive (SS163), one of the most beautiful coastal roads in the world.

☐☐ Stop 4: Positano – Italy's Most Photogenic Village

📍 Distance from Sorrento: 20 km (45-minute drive along the Amalfi Coast Road)

Positano is the crown jewel of the Amalfi Coast, with colorful cliffside houses, turquoise waters, and boutique shops. It's one of Italy's most Instagrammable destinations, but beyond its beauty, Positano offers fantastic beaches, great food, and a vibrant atmosphere.

✨ Best Things to Do in Positano

✓☐ Spiaggia Grande – The main beach, perfect for relaxing under the sun.

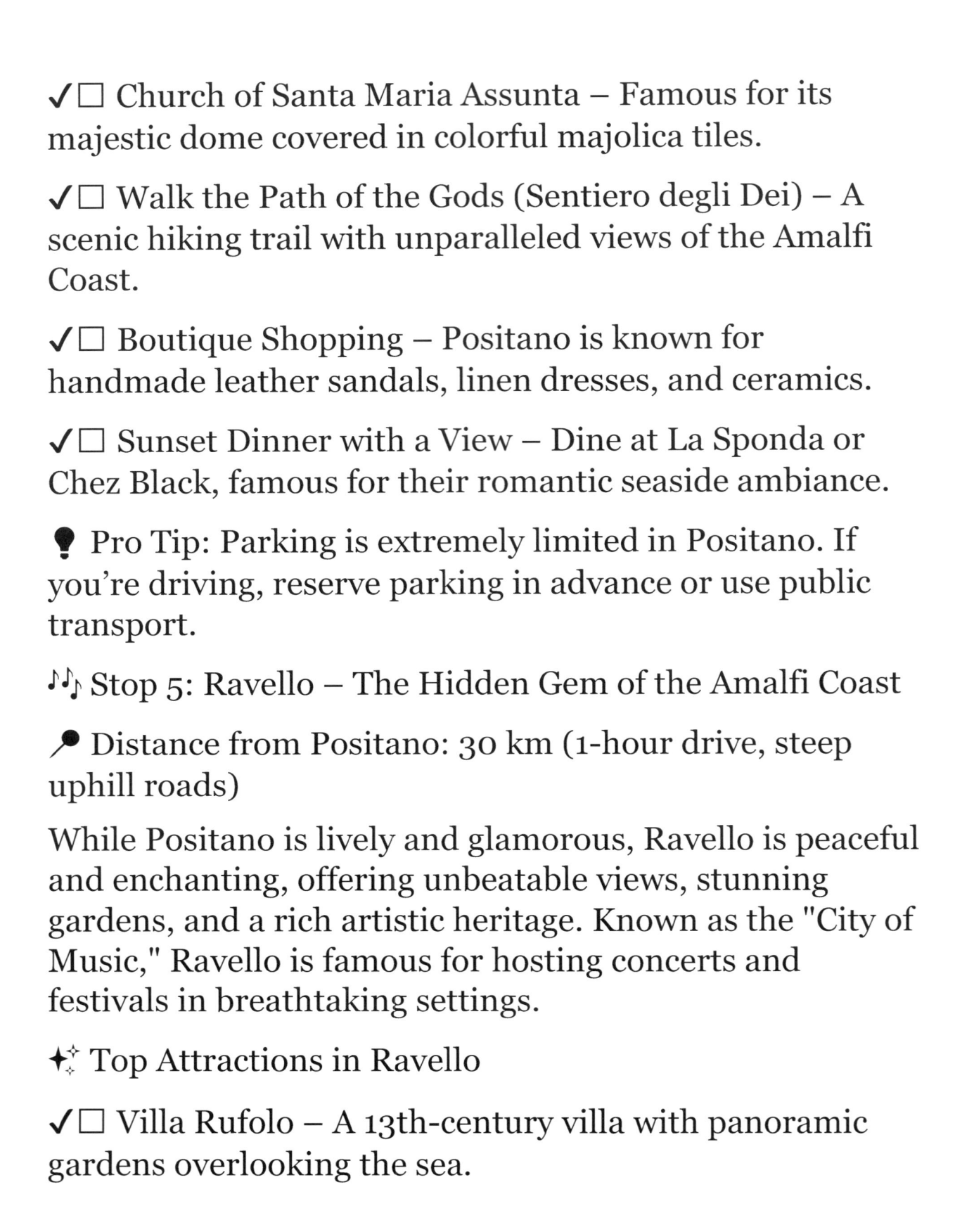

✓☐ Church of Santa Maria Assunta – Famous for its majestic dome covered in colorful majolica tiles.

✓☐ Walk the Path of the Gods (Sentiero degli Dei) – A scenic hiking trail with unparalleled views of the Amalfi Coast.

✓☐ Boutique Shopping – Positano is known for handmade leather sandals, linen dresses, and ceramics.

✓☐ Sunset Dinner with a View – Dine at La Sponda or Chez Black, famous for their romantic seaside ambiance.

💡 Pro Tip: Parking is extremely limited in Positano. If you're driving, reserve parking in advance or use public transport.

🎵 Stop 5: Ravello – The Hidden Gem of the Amalfi Coast

📍 Distance from Positano: 30 km (1-hour drive, steep uphill roads)

While Positano is lively and glamorous, Ravello is peaceful and enchanting, offering unbeatable views, stunning gardens, and a rich artistic heritage. Known as the "City of Music," Ravello is famous for hosting concerts and festivals in breathtaking settings.

✨ Top Attractions in Ravello

✓☐ Villa Rufolo – A 13th-century villa with panoramic gardens overlooking the sea.

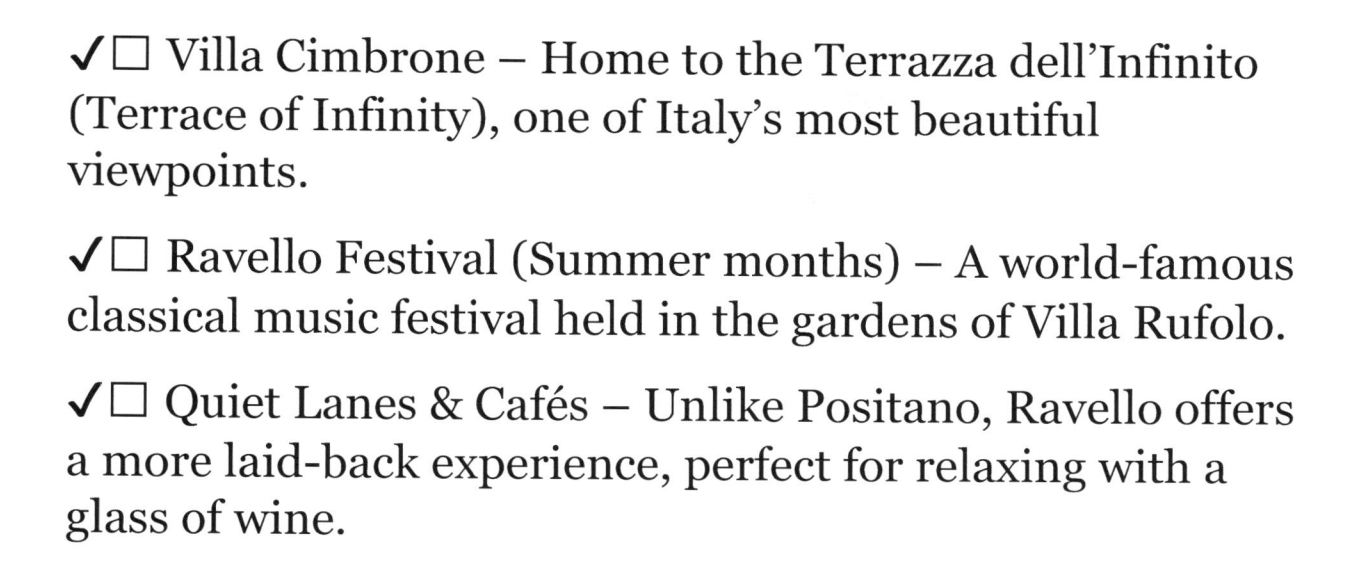

✓☐ Villa Cimbrone – Home to the Terrazza dell'Infinito (Terrace of Infinity), one of Italy's most beautiful viewpoints.

✓☐ Ravello Festival (Summer months) – A world-famous classical music festival held in the gardens of Villa Rufolo.

✓☐ Quiet Lanes & Cafés – Unlike Positano, Ravello offers a more laid-back experience, perfect for relaxing with a glass of wine.

The Puglia and Matera Heritage Route: A Journey Through Italy's Timeless South

Southern Italy is a land of contrasts, where ancient history, dramatic landscapes, and culinary excellence come together to create an unforgettable road trip experience. The Puglia and Matera Heritage Route offers travelers the chance to explore the whitewashed villages, stunning coastline, and UNESCO-listed wonders of Puglia, combined with the otherworldly cave city of Matera in Basilicata.

From the trulli houses of Alberobello to the rock-hewn churches of Matera, this journey is an exploration of Italy's lesser-known, yet equally enchanting regions.

🚗 Getting Started: Overview of the Route

📍 Starting Point: Bari, Puglia

📍 End Point: Matera, Basilicata

📏 Distance: ~300 km (5-6 days recommended for exploration)

This road trip starts in Bari, the lively capital of Puglia, before heading to the charming coastal towns, unique countryside villages, and historic landmarks of the region. It then continues inland to Matera, one of the oldest continuously inhabited cities in the world, before looping back towards the coast.

🏙️ Stop 1: Bari – The Gateway to Puglia

📍 Bari, Puglia

Before hitting the road, spend time exploring Bari, a city that perfectly blends medieval charm with a modern seaside buzz.

✨ Must-See Attractions in Bari

✅ Basilica di San Nicola – Houses the relics of Saint Nicholas (Santa Claus!) and is an important pilgrimage site.

✅ Bari Vecchia (Old Town) – A maze of narrow alleyways, historic churches, and vibrant piazzas.

✅ Lungomare di Bari – One of Italy's most scenic seaside promenades.

✓☐ Pasta Street (Strada delle Orecchiette) – Watch local women making handmade orecchiette pasta right outside their homes.

💡 Foodie Must-Try: Focaccia Barese, a crispy flatbread topped with cherry tomatoes, olives, and oregano.

🏔 Stop 2: Polignano a Mare – The Jewel of Puglia's Coast

📍 Distance from Bari: 35 km (~35-minute drive)

Polignano a Mare is one of Puglia's most breathtaking coastal towns, famous for its white cliffs, dramatic sea caves, and turquoise waters.

✨ Best Things to Do in Polignano a Mare

✓☐ Lama Monachile Beach – A stunning beach nestled between cliffs, perfect for a swim or scenic photo.

✓☐ Grotta Palazzese – A world-famous restaurant set inside a natural cave overlooking the sea.

✓☐ Domenico Modugno Statue – Dedicated to the singer of "Volare," one of Italy's most famous songs.

💡 Pro Tip: Arrive early in the morning to enjoy the beach without the crowds.

🏠 Stop 3: Alberobello – The Fairytale Village of Trulli

📍 Distance from Polignano a Mare: 30 km (~40-minute drive)

Alberobello is a UNESCO World Heritage Site, famous for its trulli houses, unique white stone dwellings with conical roofs.

✨ Must-See Attractions in Alberobello

✓☐ Rione Monti – The main trulli district, filled with picturesque streets and charming souvenir shops.

✓☐ Trullo Sovrano – The only two-story trullo, now a museum.

✓☐ Church of Saint Anthony – A trullo-style church, blending religion and tradition.

💡 Travel Tip: For an authentic stay, book a night in a trullo B&B for a truly unique experience.

🍷 Stop 4: Locorotondo and Martina Franca – Puglia's Wine & Baroque Towns

📍 Distance from Alberobello: 10-15 km (~20-minute drive)

Next, explore the whitewashed town of Locorotondo, famous for its circular layout and wine production, and Martina Franca, known for its Baroque architecture.

✨ What to Do in Locorotondo & Martina Franca

✓☐ Wine tasting in Locorotondo – The town is famous for white wines, best enjoyed at a local vineyard.

✓☐ Historic Center of Martina Franca – Wander through ornate Baroque palaces and charming piazzas.

✓☐ Try Capocollo di Martina Franca – A delicious cured meat unique to this region.

☐☐ Stop 5: Ostuni – The White City

📍 Distance from Martina Franca: 25 km (~35-minute drive)

Perched on a hill with views of the Adriatic Sea, Ostuni is a brilliantly whitewashed city, often called "La Città Bianca" (The White City).

✦ Top Attractions in Ostuni

✓☐ Ostuni Cathedral – A mix of Gothic and Romanesque architecture.

✓☐ Piazza della Libertà – The heart of the town, filled with cafés and local boutiques.

✓☐ Olive Grove Tours – Puglia is home to some of the oldest olive trees in Italy, producing world-class olive oil.

💡 Must-Try Dish: Orecchiette con Cime di Rapa – A traditional Puglian pasta dish with broccoli rabe, garlic, and anchovies.

☐☐ Stop 6: Matera – Italy's Ancient Cave City

📍 Distance from Ostuni: 110 km (~1.5-hour drive)

Saving the best for last, Matera is a UNESCO World Heritage Site and one of the oldest continuously inhabited cities in the world. The Sassi di Matera (ancient cave dwellings) create a surreal, almost biblical atmosphere, making this one of Italy's most unique destinations.

✨ Top Things to See in Matera

✓☐ Sassi di Matera – Wander through centuries-old cave dwellings, churches, and monasteries.

✓☐ Casa Grotta di Vico Solitario – A reconstructed cave house, showing what life was like in Matera centuries ago.

✓☐ Belvedere Murgia Timone – The best viewpoint overlooking Matera.

✓☐ Rock Churches (Chiese Rupestri) – Stunning ancient churches carved directly into the rock, some with frescoes dating back to the Middle Ages.

💡 Did You Know? Matera was the filming location for James Bond's No Time to Die and Mel Gibson's The Passion of the Christ.

Exploring the Heart of Southern Italy: Bari, Alberobello, Matera & Gargano

Southern Italy is a region filled with historical wonders, architectural marvels, and breathtaking coastal landscapes. The Puglia and Basilicata regions, in particular, offer an unforgettable blend of ancient history, unique architecture, and stunning natural beauty.

From the bustling port city of Bari to the fairytale-like trulli houses of Alberobello, and from the ancient cave dwellings of Matera to the hidden coastal treasures of Gargano National Park, this road trip promises a rich cultural and scenic adventure.

Let's dive into this journey through Italy's timeless south!

🚘 Stop 1: Bari – The Gateway to Puglia

📍 Bari, Puglia

Bari, the capital of Puglia, is a vibrant city that blends history, tradition, and modern life. As a major port city on the Adriatic Sea, it serves as a starting point for many road trips through southern Italy.

✨ Must-See Attractions in Bari

✓☐ Basilica di San Nicola – A stunning Romanesque church that houses the relics of Saint Nicholas (yes, Santa Claus!).

✓☐ Bari Vecchia (Old Town) – A maze of narrow, stone-paved streets filled with historic buildings and lively piazzas.

✓☐ Pasta Street (Strada delle Orecchiette) – A charming alley where local women make orecchiette pasta by hand.

✓☐ Castello Normanno-Svevo – A 12th-century castle with incredible medieval architecture.

✓☐ Lungomare di Bari – One of Italy's longest and most scenic seaside promenades.

💡 Foodie Tip: Try sgagliozze (fried polenta squares) and panzerotti (fried dough filled with mozzarella and tomato).

🏠 Stop 2: Alberobello – The Fairytale Village of Trulli

📍 Distance from Bari: 55 km (~1-hour drive)

Alberobello is a UNESCO World Heritage Site famous for its trulli houses, small whitewashed stone buildings with conical roofs that make the town look like something out of a storybook.

✨ Best Things to See in Alberobello

✓☐ Rione Monti – The most famous area filled with over 1,000 trulli, now used as homes, shops, and restaurants.

✓☐ Trullo Sovrano – The only two-story trullo, now a museum showcasing how families once lived.

✓☐ Church of Saint Anthony – A trullo-style church, making it one of the most unique places of worship in Italy.

✓☐ Aia Piccola – A quieter area with authentic trulli still used as homes.

💡 Travel Tip: Stay overnight in a trullo hotel for a one-of-a-kind experience!

☐☐ Stop 3: Matera – Italy's Ancient Cave City

📍 Distance from Alberobello: 70 km (~1.5-hour drive)

One of the world's oldest cities still in continuous habitation is Matera, which is situated in the Basilicata area. The Sassi di Matera, a complex of ancient cave dwellings, has been carved into the rock for over 9,000 years.

✨ What to Explore in Matera

✓☐ Sassi di Matera – Walk through centuries-old cave dwellings, churches, and monasteries.

✓☐ Casa Grotta di Vico Solitario – A reconstructed cave house that gives a glimpse of past life.

✓☐ Belvedere Murgia Timone – The best viewpoint overlooking Matera, especially stunning at sunset.

✓☐ Chiesa Rupestre di Santa Maria de Idris – A rock-hewn church with ancient frescoes.

✓☐ Palombaro Lungo – A giant underground cistern that once supplied the city with water.

💡 **Did You Know?** Matera was a filming location for James Bond's No Time to Die and Mel Gibson's The Passion of the Christ.

💡 **Stay Overnight:** Book a night in a cave hotel for a truly immersive experience.

🌊 **Stop 4: Gargano National Park – Puglia's Hidden Coastal Gem**

📍 **Distance from Matera:** 230 km (~3-hour drive)

Located in northern Puglia, Gargano National Park is one of Italy's most stunning natural treasures, offering secluded beaches, white limestone cliffs, dense forests, and charming coastal villages.

✨ **Must-See Places in Gargano**

✓☐ **Vieste** – A beautiful seaside town with whitewashed houses, narrow alleys, and stunning views.

✓☐ **Pizzomunno Rock** – A massive limestone monolith rising from the sea near Vieste's beach.

✓☐ **Baia delle Zagare** – A breathtaking hidden beach with turquoise waters and sea stacks.

✓☐ **Foresta Umbra** – A lush forest filled with ancient beech trees, perfect for hiking.

✓☐ Monte Sant'Angelo – A UNESCO-listed town famous for the Sanctuary of St. Michael the Archangel.

💡 Outdoor Adventure: Rent a boat to explore the hidden sea caves and rock arches along the coast.

Sicily's Grand Tour: A Journey Through Italy's Enchanting Island

Sicily is a world of its own—an island where history, culture, nature, and cuisine blend into an unforgettable road trip experience. From Palermo's historic streets to Catania's Baroque beauty, from the volcanic landscapes of Mount Etna to the crystal-clear waters of the Aeolian Islands, every stop on this journey offers something unique.

With ancient Greek ruins, medieval villages, sun-drenched beaches, and mouthwatering food, this Sicilian Grand Tour will take you through some of the island's most breathtaking and culturally rich destinations.

🚗 Stop 1: Palermo – The Historic Capital of Sicily

📍 Palermo, Northern Sicily

The journey begins in Palermo, the beating heart of Sicily and one of Italy's most fascinating cities. This vibrant capital is a mix of Arab, Norman, and Baroque influences, reflected in its architecture, street food, and lively atmosphere.

✦ Must-Visit Attractions in Palermo

✓☐ Palermo Cathedral – A stunning blend of Norman, Gothic, and Baroque styles.

✓☐ Norman Palace & Palatine Chapel – Home to golden Byzantine mosaics and a rich royal history.

✓☐ Ballarò & Vucciria Markets – Bustling street food markets where you can sample authentic Sicilian flavors.

✓☐ Teatro Massimo – One of Europe's grandest opera houses, known from The Godfather Part III.

✓☐ Mondello Beach – A short drive away, this paradise beach offers turquoise waters and golden sand.

💡 Foodie Tip: Try arancini (fried rice balls), pane con la milza (spleen sandwich), and cannoli (crispy pastry filled with sweet ricotta).

🚗 Next Stop: Cefalù – 70 km (~1-hour drive)

☐☐ Stop 2: Cefalù – A Coastal Gem

📍 Northern Sicily

Cefalù is a charming seaside town famous for its golden beaches, medieval streets, and historic Norman cathedral.

✦ Highlights of Cefalù

✓☐ Cefalù Cathedral – A magnificent Norman church with stunning mosaics.

✓☐ Lungomare Beach – One of Sicily's best beaches, perfect for swimming and sunbathing.

✓☐ La Rocca – A rocky cliff offering panoramic views over the town and sea.

💡 Local Dish to Try: Pasta alla Norma (pasta with eggplant, tomatoes, and ricotta salata).

🚗 Next Stop: Taormina – 180 km (~3-hour drive)

🌋 Stop 3: Taormina & Mount Etna – Sicily's Volcanic Beauty

📍 Eastern Sicily

Taormina is a postcard-perfect hilltop town overlooking the Ionian Sea. With its ancient Greek ruins, luxurious villas, and stunning coastal views, it is one of Sicily's most glamorous destinations.

✨ What to See in Taormina

✓☐ Ancient Greek Theatre – One of the most scenic amphitheaters in the world, with views of Mount Etna and the sea.

✓☐ Corso Umberto – The town's lively main street filled with boutiques, cafés, and historic buildings.

✓☐ Isola Bella – A small island and nature reserve, perfect for a refreshing swim.

🌋 Exploring Mount Etna

📍 Distance from Taormina: 60 km (~1.5-hour drive)

Mount Etna, Europe's highest and most active volcano, is a must-visit for adventurers and nature lovers.

💡 Best Ways to Explore Mount Etna:

✓□ Take a guided Jeep tour to the lava fields and craters.

✓□ Ride the cable car to 2,500 meters and hike to the summit.

✓□ Visit local wineries producing Etna DOC wines.

🚗 Next Stop: Catania – 50 km (~1-hour drive)

□□ Stop 4: Catania – The Baroque Beauty of Sicily

📍 Eastern Sicily

Catania is a vibrant port city famous for its lava-stone Baroque architecture, bustling markets, and lively nightlife.

✨ Top Attractions in Catania

✓□ Piazza del Duomo & Elephant Fountain – The heart of the city, with an iconic lava-stone elephant statue.

✓□ Catania Fish Market – A lively traditional fish market, full of Sicilian character.

✓☐ Via Etnea – The city's main shopping street, with views of Mount Etna.

✓☐ Castello Ursino – A 13th-century fortress built from black lava stone.

💡 Must-Try Dish: Pasta con le sarde (pasta with sardines, wild fennel, and pine nuts).

🚗 Next Stop: Aeolian Islands – Take a ferry from Milazzo (~1-hour drive from Catania)

⛴ Stop 5: The Aeolian Islands – Sicily's Hidden Paradise

📍 Northern Sicily (Island Group in the Tyrrhenian Sea)

The Aeolian Islands, a UNESCO-listed archipelago, are a perfect getaway for beach lovers, hikers, and adventure seekers.

☐☐ Best Islands to Visit

✓☐ Lipari – The largest island, with beautiful beaches, historic castles, and a lively town.

✓☐ Stromboli – Home to an active volcano, where you can hike to see lava eruptions at night.

✓☐ Salina – A lush green island known for its capers, Malvasia wine, and stunning hiking trails.

✓☐ Panarea – The jet-set island, with luxury villas, whitewashed houses, and chic nightlife.

💡 Outdoor Activities: Snorkeling, boat tours, and volcano trekking.

🚗 Final Stop: Drive back to Palermo to complete the loop (~2.5-hour ferry + 3-hour drive).

☐☐ Best Local Sicilian Dishes to Try

Sicilian food is a fusion of Greek, Arab, Spanish, and Italian influences, making it one of the most diverse cuisines in Italy.

✓☐ Arancini – Fried rice balls stuffed with ragù, cheese, or spinach.

✓☐ Caponata – A sweet and sour eggplant stew with olives and capers.

✓☐ Cannoli – A crispy pastry filled with sweet ricotta.

✓☐ Granita & Brioche – A refreshing Sicilian-style sorbet served with soft bread.

✓☐ Sfincione – A Sicilian-style pizza with tomato sauce, onions, and anchovies.

Naples

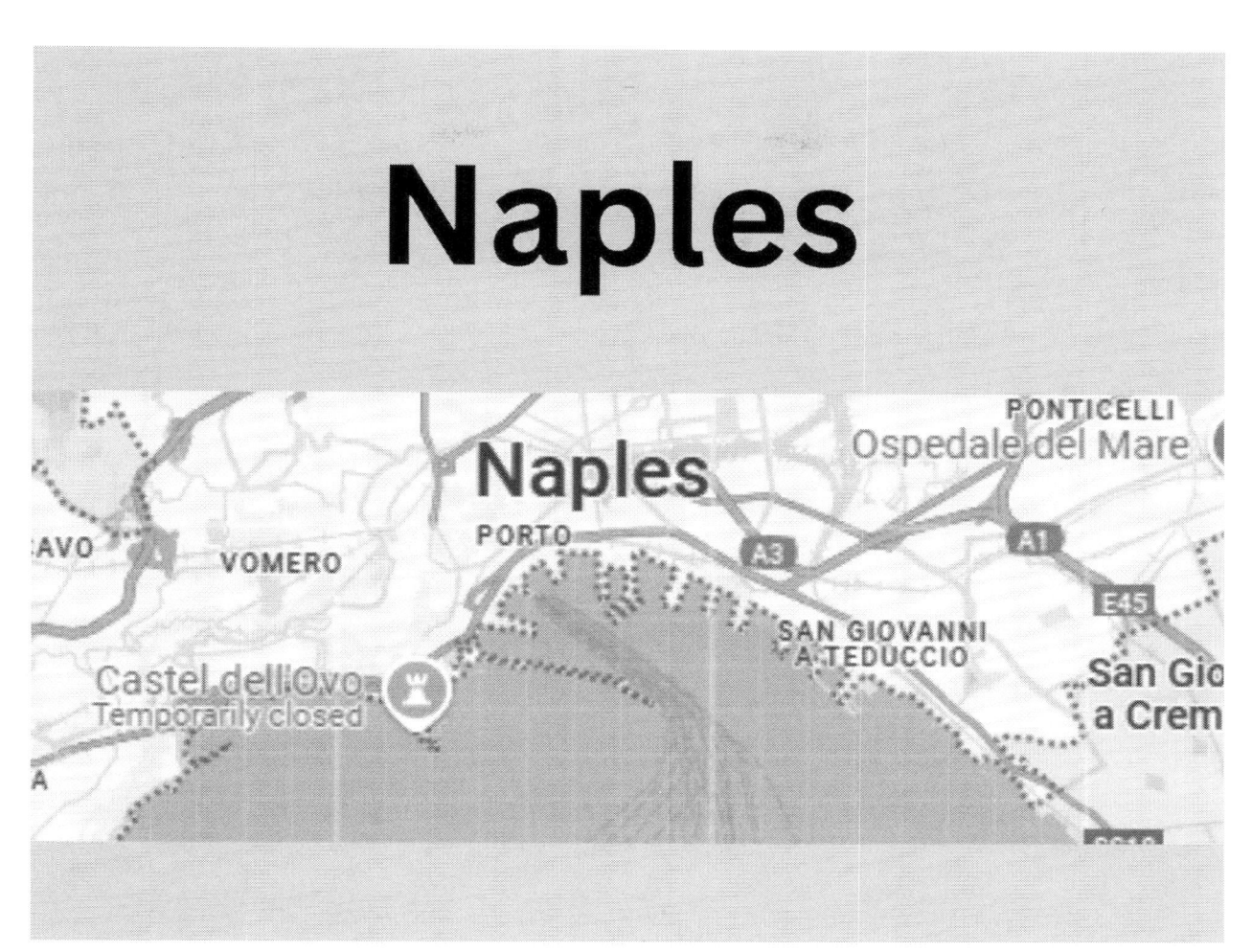

SCAN HERE

HOW TO USE QR CODE
- Open your phone's camera app or download scanner app from play store or app store
- point the camera at the QR code for a few seconds (no need to take a phone)
- A link should appear on the display leading you the location of the code

Sorrento

SCAN HERE

HOW TO USE QR CODE

- Open your phone's camera app or download scanner app from play store or app store
- point the camera at the QR code for a few seconds (no need to take a phone)
- A link should appear on the display leading you the location of the code

Positano

SCAN HERE

HOW TO USE QR CODE
- Open your phone's camera app or download scanner app from play store or app store
- point the camera at the QR code for a few seconds (no need to take a phone)
- A link should appear on the display leading you the location of the code

Ravello

SCAN HERE

HOW TO USE QR CODE
- Open your phone's camera app or download scanner app from play store or app store
- point the camera at the QR code for a few seconds (no need to take a phone)
- A link should appear on the display leading you the location of the code

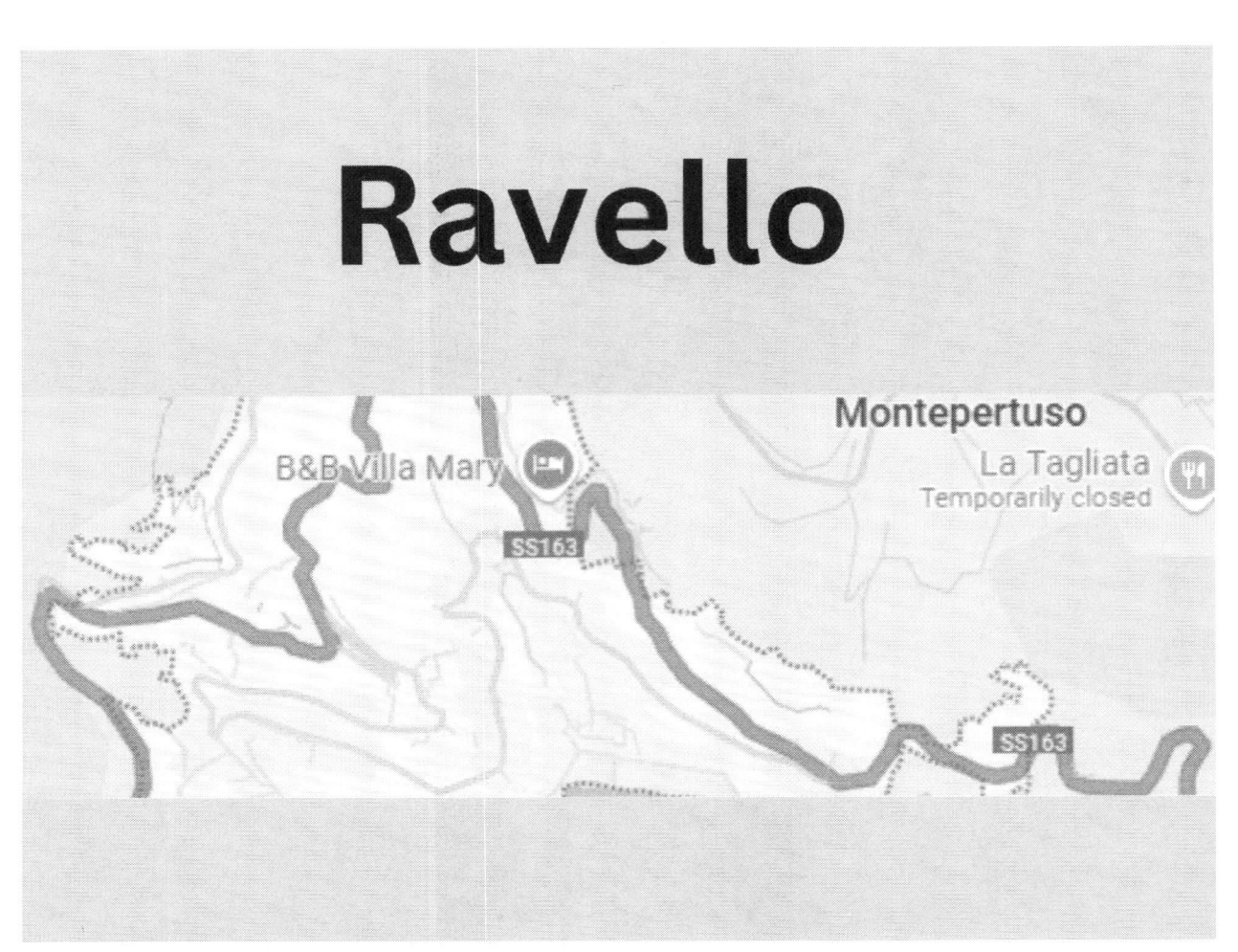

Ostuni

SCAN HERE

HOW TO USE QR CODE

- Open your phone's camera app or download scanner app from play store or app store
- point the camera at the QR code for a few seconds (no need to take a phone)
- A link should appear on the display leading you the location of the code

Ostuni

SCAN HERE

HOW TO USE QR CODE
- Open your phone's camera app or download scanner app from play store or app store
- point the camera at the QR code for a few seconds (no need to take a phone)
- A link should appear on the display leading you the location of the code

Alberobell

SCAN HERE

HOW TO USE QR CODE
- Open your phone's camera app or download scanner app from play store or app store
- point the camera at the QR code for a few seconds (no need to take a phone)
- A link should appear on the display leading you the location of the code

CHAPTER SIX

Hidden Gems and Lesser-Known Routes

Italy is famous for its iconic road trips, but beyond the well-trodden paths of Tuscany, the Amalfi Coast, and the Dolomites, there are hidden gems and lesser-known routes waiting to be explored. This chapter unveils Italy's best-kept secrets, offering a chance to escape the crowds and discover breathtaking landscapes, medieval villages, and untouched coastal retreats.

Whether you prefer a scenic coastal drive along rugged cliffs and crystal-clear waters or a winding journey through dramatic mountain terrain, these off-the-beaten-path destinations will add a unique touch to your Italian road trip experience.

🚗 Exploring Off-the-Beaten-Path Destinations

While Florence, Venice, and Rome remain Italy's star attractions, there are countless lesser-known towns and regions that offer equally stunning landscapes, rich history, and authentic experiences.

Here are some of Italy's best hidden gems to add to your road trip itinerary:

❈ 1. The Langhe and Monferrato Wine Route (Piedmont)

📍 Region: Northern Italy

Best for: Wine lovers, foodies, countryside landscapes

This underrated alternative to Tuscany is a paradise for wine enthusiasts and slow travelers. The Langhe, Roero, and Monferrato regions are home to rolling vineyards, charming villages, and some of Italy's finest wines, including Barolo and Barbaresco.

✦ Must-Visit Stops:

✓☐ La Morra – A hilltop town offering breathtaking views of the vineyards.

✓☐ Barolo – The birthplace of the famous Barolo wine, with historic wine cellars to visit.

✓☐ Alba – The truffle capital of Italy, known for its white truffle festival in autumn.

✓☐ Acqui Terme – A spa town with ancient Roman baths and natural hot springs.

💡 Hidden Gem: Try a wine tasting at a family-run vineyard for an authentic experience.

🚗 Next Stop: Drive south to Liguria's hidden coastal villages.

🐚 2. The Riviera di Levante: Liguria's Secret Coastline

📍 Region: Northwestern Italy

Best for: Coastal views, beach lovers, seafood

While Cinque Terre and Portofino draw thousands of visitors each year, Liguria's eastern coastline (Riviera di Levante) remains a hidden treasure. This stunning coastal drive takes you through secluded coves, colorful fishing villages, and dramatic cliffs.

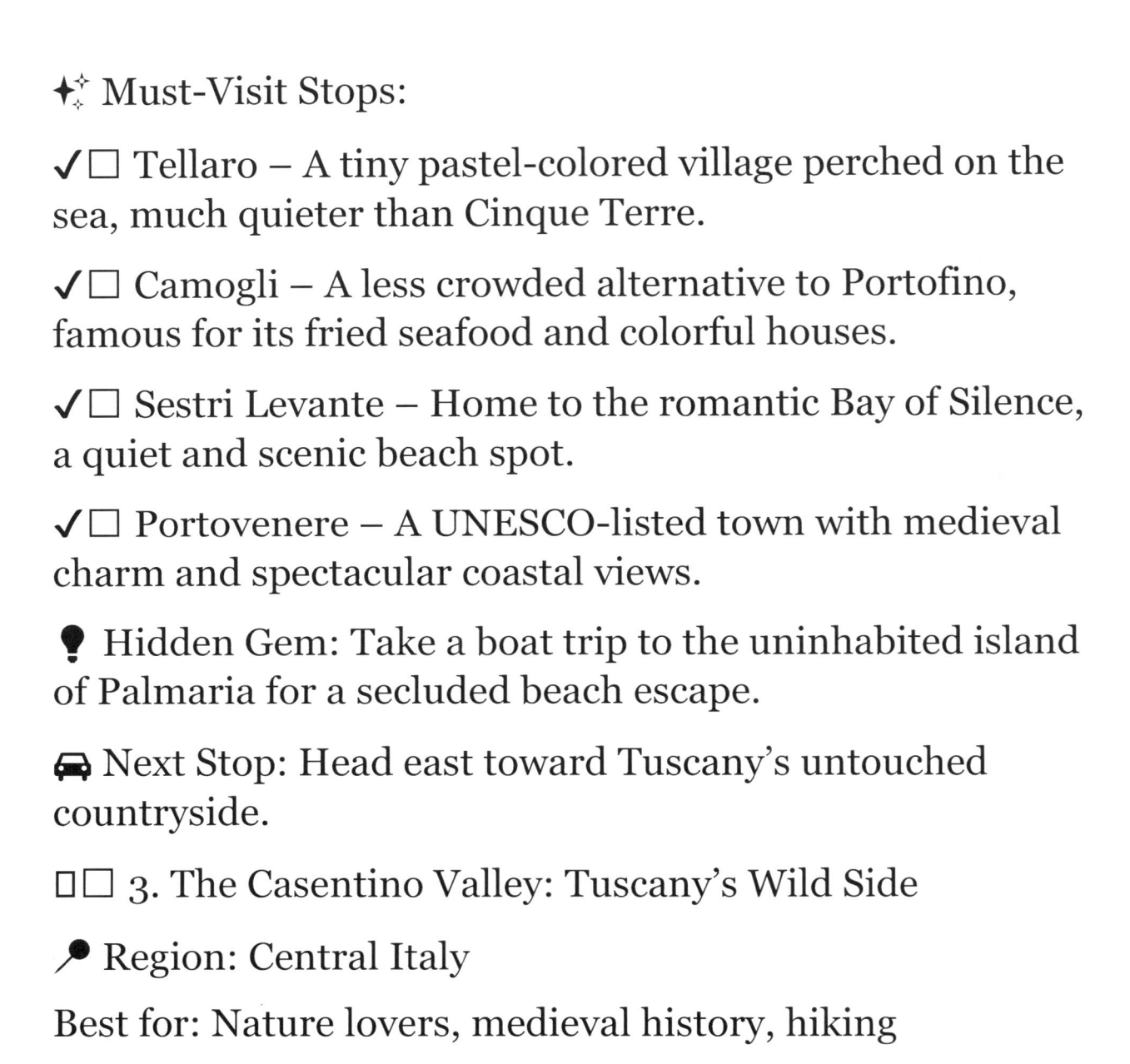

✨ Must-Visit Stops:

✓☐ Tellaro – A tiny pastel-colored village perched on the sea, much quieter than Cinque Terre.

✓☐ Camogli – A less crowded alternative to Portofino, famous for its fried seafood and colorful houses.

✓☐ Sestri Levante – Home to the romantic Bay of Silence, a quiet and scenic beach spot.

✓☐ Portovenere – A UNESCO-listed town with medieval charm and spectacular coastal views.

💡 Hidden Gem: Take a boat trip to the uninhabited island of Palmaria for a secluded beach escape.

🚗 Next Stop: Head east toward Tuscany's untouched countryside.

☐☐ 3. The Casentino Valley: Tuscany's Wild Side

📍 Region: Central Italy

Best for: Nature lovers, medieval history, hiking

Tuscany is known for its rolling vineyards and Renaissance cities, but Casentino Valley is its best-kept secret. Nestled between Florence and Arezzo, this region offers forests, ancient monasteries, and untouched medieval villages.

✦ Must-Visit Stops:

✓☐ Poppi – A hilltop town with the beautiful Castello di Poppi, offering panoramic views.

✓☐ Camaldoli Monastery – A remote Benedictine monastery surrounded by forests.

✓☐ La Verna Sanctuary – A peaceful retreat where St. Francis of Assisi lived, offering stunning mountain scenery.

✓☐ Foreste Casentinesi National Park – One of Italy's most pristine national parks, ideal for hiking and wildlife spotting.

💡 Hidden Gem: Visit in autumn to experience Tuscany's most spectacular fall foliage.

🚗 Next Stop: Travel south toward the hidden beaches of Lazio.

☐☐ 4. The Secret Beaches of Lazio and the Ulysses Coast

📍 Region: Central Italy

Best for: Secluded beaches, history, coastal scenery

Most visitors to Lazio head straight to Rome, but just a short drive south, the Ulysses Coast hides some of Italy's most beautiful and undiscovered beaches.

✨ Must-Visit Stops:

✓☐ Sperlonga – A whitewashed village with golden beaches and ancient Roman caves.

✓☐ Gaeta – Home to stunning coastal cliffs, medieval forts, and hidden sea grottoes.

✓☐ San Felice Circeo – A secluded beach paradise with crystal-clear waters and rocky coves.

✓☐ Terracina – A charming seaside town with Roman ruins and panoramic views of the Mediterranean.

💡 Hidden Gem: Visit the Temple of Jupiter Anxur, an ancient Roman temple with spectacular sea views.

🚗 Next Stop: Drive south into the rugged landscapes of Calabria.

☐☐ 5. The Aspromonte and Sila Mountains (Calabria)

📍 Region: Southern Italy

Best for: Adventure seekers, mountain drives, ancient villages

Calabria, the toe of Italy's boot, is often overlooked by tourists, making it one of Italy's last true hidden gems. With mountain roads, deep gorges, and ancient hilltop towns, this route offers an unforgettable experience for those seeking rugged beauty and authenticity.

✦ Must-Visit Stops:

✓☐ Gerace – A stunning medieval village with a Norman castle and breathtaking mountain views.

✓☐ Scilla – A mythical fishing town, known as the home of the sea monster Scylla from Greek mythology.

✓☐ Aspromonte National Park – A dramatic mountain range, ideal for hiking and scenic drives.

✓☐ Sila National Park – A high-altitude forested plateau, perfect for outdoor adventures and food lovers.

💡 Hidden Gem: Try Calabria's famous 'nduja—a spicy, spreadable pork sausage unique to this region.

🚘 Next Stop: Travel to Sicily for an off-the-beaten-path island experience.

🏔 Scenic Coastal Routes vs. Mountain Drives: Which One to Choose?

If you love coastal scenery:

🌊 Best Coastal Routes:

✓☐ Riviera di Levante (Liguria) – Dramatic cliffs and colorful villages

✓☐ Ulysses Coast (Lazio) – Secluded Mediterranean beaches

✓☐ Costa Viola (Calabria) – Stunning sea views and hidden coves

If you prefer mountain adventures:

☐☐ Best Mountain Drives:

✓☐ Casentino Valley (Tuscany) – Lush forests and medieval villages

✓☐ Sila National Park (Calabria) – Rugged mountains and untouched nature

✓☐ Dolomiti Friulane (Friuli-Venezia Giulia) – Dramatic peaks and Alpine scenery

Best Villages and Countryside Retreats

Italy's countryside is dotted with picturesque villages, medieval hamlets, and serene retreats, offering a peaceful escape from the hustle and bustle of city life. While famous towns like San Gimignano and Positano attract large crowds, there are lesser-known villages that remain untouched by mass tourism.

Whether you're looking for charming stone-built villages, vineyard-covered hills, or stunning mountain retreats, these hidden gems provide the perfect blend of history, culture, and breathtaking landscapes.

🏠 . Civita di Bagnoregio, also known as the "Dying Town" in Lazio

📍 Region: Lazio

Best for: A unique and surreal experience

Perched atop a crumbling hill in central Italy, Civita di Bagnoregio is a fairytale-like village that seems frozen in time. Known as the "Dying Town" due to the gradual erosion of the rock beneath it, this car-free village is accessible only via a pedestrian bridge.

✨ Why Visit?

✓☐ Incredible panoramic views over the Tiber Valley.

✓☐ Ancient stone houses and cobbled streets untouched for centuries.

✓☐ Peaceful atmosphere, perfect for a quiet countryside retreat.

💡 Hidden Gem: Visit in the early morning or late evening to experience its mystical beauty without crowds.

🚗 Next Stop: Drive toward Tuscany for a vineyard retreat.

❈ 2. Brisighella (Emilia-Romagna) – A Colorful Medieval Gem

📍 Region: Emilia-Romagna

Best for: Food lovers, medieval history, scenic landscapes

Nestled between rolling green hills and olive groves, Brisighella is a colorful medieval village with a slow-paced lifestyle. It is famous for its high-quality olive oil, local wine, and charming pastel-colored houses.

✦ Why Visit?

✓☐ Climb the Clock Tower for panoramic views of the surrounding countryside.

✓☐ Explore the Via degli Asini, an ancient covered walkway carved into the rock.

✓☐ Taste the famous Brisighella olive oil, considered one of the best in Italy.

💡 Hidden Gem: Take a scenic drive through the Apennine Mountains for breathtaking landscapes.

🚗 Next Stop: Travel south toward Umbria's hidden treasures.

☐☐ 3. Castelluccio di Norcia (Umbria) – Italy's Most Scenic Plateau

📍 Region: Umbria

Best for: Nature lovers, photography, hiking

At 1,452 meters above sea level, Castelluccio di Norcia is one of Italy's highest and most beautiful villages. Located in the heart of the Sibillini Mountains, this village is best known for the Fiorita (flowering season) when the surrounding fields burst into a kaleidoscope of colors.

✦ **Why Visit?**

✓☐ Breathtaking mountain landscapes, perfect for hiking and photography.

✓☐ Fiorita Festival (May–July) – A natural spectacle of blooming wildflowers.

✓☐ Try the famous local lentils, a specialty of this region.

💡 Hidden Gem: Drive the Grande Anello dei Sibillini, a scenic mountain road with jaw-dropping views.

🚗 Next Stop: Head east toward the Adriatic Coast for a seaside retreat.

☐☐ 4. Pietrapertosa (Basilicata) – Italy's Highest Village

📍 Region: Basilicata

Best for: Adventure seekers, dramatic landscapes

Tucked into the rocky Lucanian Dolomites, Pietrapertosa is one of Italy's most unique villages, seemingly carved directly into the mountains. This remote and breathtaking spot is perfect for those seeking adventure and authentic local culture.

✦ **Why Visit?**

✓☐ Walk the Via Ferrata delle Dolomiti Lucane, a thrilling mountain hiking route.

✓☐ Experience the Volo dell'Angelo (Flight of the Angel), one of the world's most extreme zip lines.

✓☐ Explore the Saracen fortress, offering panoramic views over the valley.

💡 Hidden Gem: Visit Castelmezzano, a neighboring village, and take the twin zip line ride between the two villages.

🚗 Next Stop: Travel west toward Calabria's ghost towns.

🏰 Unique Road Trip Experiences

Italy is filled with mystical and unusual destinations that make for a truly unforgettable road trip. From abandoned ghost towns to natural thermal baths and centuries-old castles, here are some of the most unique road trip experiences in Italy.

👻 1. The Ghost Town of Craco (Basilicata)

📍 Region: Basilicata

Best for: History lovers, eerie landscapes

Craco is one of Italy's most famous abandoned ghost towns, dramatically perched on a hilltop. This once-thriving medieval village was completely abandoned in the 1960s due to landslides, leaving behind a hauntingly beautiful ruin.

✨ Why Visit?

✓☐ Walk through empty stone buildings frozen in time.

✓☐ Feel the spooky yet fascinating atmosphere of a deserted town.

✓☐ Explore one of Italy's most famous movie locations (featured in "The Passion of the Christ").

💡 Hidden Gem: Visit at sunset for a truly otherworldly experience.

🚗 Next Stop: Relax at nearby natural hot springs.

♨☐ 2. Saturnia Hot Springs (Tuscany) – Italy's Natural Thermal Baths

📍 Region: Tuscany

Best for: Relaxation, wellness, natural beauty

The Saturnia Hot Springs are one of Italy's most stunning natural wonders, featuring steaming turquoise pools formed by cascading waterfalls. These thermal baths have been used since Roman times for their healing properties.

✨ Why Visit?

✓☐ Relax in 37°C (98°F) mineral-rich waters with a stunning natural backdrop.

✓☐ Enjoy a free and open-air thermal experience.

✓☐ Experience one of Italy's most photogenic spots.

💡 Hidden Gem: Visit in the early morning or late evening to avoid crowds and enjoy the most peaceful experience.

🚗 Next Stop: Travel to a nearby medieval hill town for a countryside retreat.

🏰 3. The Fairytale Castles of Trentino-Alto Adige

📍 Region: Northern Italy

Best for: Fairytale lovers, history, photography

Italy isn't just about Roman ruins—it's also home to some of Europe's most enchanting castles. The Trentino-Alto Adige region is filled with fairytale-like fortresses set against dramatic mountain landscapes.

✨ Must-Visit Castles:

✓☐ Castel Tirolo – A stunning medieval castle with breathtaking views of the Alps.

✓☐ Castel Roncolo – Known for its frescoes depicting medieval life.

✓☐ Castel Beseno – One of Italy's largest fortified castles, offering an immersive medieval experience.

💡 Hidden Gem: Stay overnight in a castle hotel for a truly magical experience.

🚗 Next Stop: Drive toward the Dolomites for another scenic adventure.

ITALY

CHAPTER SEVEN

Practical Road Trip Tips and Resources

Planning and executing a successful road trip in Italy requires more than just choosing the best routes and destinations. To ensure a smooth and stress-free journey, it's crucial to be prepared with emergency contacts, reliable navigation tools, and essential travel apps.

In this chapter, we cover roadside assistance services, emergency numbers, and must-have apps for navigation, parking, and fuel stations.

🚨 Roadside Assistance and Emergency Numbers

While Italy is known for its well-maintained roads and scenic highways, unexpected breakdowns or emergencies can still happen. Whether you need help with a flat tire, a dead battery, or an accident, knowing who to call can make all the difference.

📞 Important Emergency Numbers in Italy

☐ Police (Carabinieri & Polizia Stradale) – 112

🚑 Medical Emergency (Ambulance) – 118

🔥 Fire Department (Vigili del Fuoco) – 115

[SOS] Roadside Assistance (ACI – Automobile Club d'Italia) – 803 116

☐ ANAS Road Assistance (for highways and state roads) – 800 841 148

💡 Pro Tip: If you're a traveler from the EU, you can also dial 112, the universal emergency number, which will connect you to the appropriate service.

☐ Roadside Assistance Services

If you're renting a car in Italy, your rental company should provide roadside assistance. However, if you're driving your own vehicle, it's wise to have a backup plan. Here are the main roadside assistance providers:

🚗 ACI (Automobile Club d'Italia) – 803 116

✅ Italy's largest roadside assistance provider

✅ Offers 24/7 emergency service

✅ Covers breakdowns, towing, fuel delivery, and lockout assistance

✅ Membership required for full benefits (can be purchased for short-term travelers)

💡 How to Use It? If you don't have an ACI membership, you can still call 803 116 and pay for assistance on the spot.

☐ ANAS (Italian Road Agency) – 800 841 148

✅ Assists with issues on state roads and highways

✅ Reports road closures, landslides, and traffic incidents

✅ Free service for all drivers

💡 How to Use It? Dial 800 841 148 for updates on road conditions and emergencies.

📲 Essential Apps for Navigation, Parking, and Fuel Stations

Technology makes road-tripping in Italy easier than ever. Here are the must-have apps for a seamless journey:

🔹 Best Navigation Apps

1️⃣ Google Maps

✔️ Reliable for real-time traffic updates and navigation

✔️ Works offline if maps are downloaded in advance

✔️ Shows speed limits and alternative routes

2️⃣ Waze

✔️ Best for live traffic updates and road alerts

✔️ Alerts for speed cameras, road hazards, and police checkpoints

✔️ Community-driven for up-to-the-minute traffic reports

3️⃣ TomTom GO Navigation

✓☐ Great for detailed offline maps

✓☐ Avoids toll roads if selected in settings

✓☐ Includes speed camera alerts

💡 Pro Tip: Always have at least two navigation apps downloaded in case one doesn't work due to poor signal.

🅿☐ Best Parking Apps

It might be difficult to get parking in Italy, particularly in large cities. Use these apps to find available parking spots and avoid fines:

1☐☐ EasyPark

✓☐ Works in over 150 cities across Italy

✓☐ Allows remote parking payment via smartphone

✓☐ Sends alerts when your parking time is about to expire

2☐☐ MyCicero

✓☐ Covers parking, public transport, and train tickets

✓☐ Works in Rome, Milan, Florence, and more

✓☐ Helps locate parking garages and street parking

3☐☐ Parclick

✓☐ Best for booking parking spots in advance

✓□ Great for long-term parking in major cities

✓□ Saves money by offering discounted parking rates

💡 Pro Tip: In small towns, look for "P" signs indicating parking lots. Many areas have ZTL (limited traffic zones) where you cannot park without a permit.

⛽ Best Fuel Station Apps

Fuel prices in Italy can vary greatly between stations. These apps help find the best fuel prices and nearest charging stations for electric vehicles:

1□□ Prezzi Benzina

✓□ Best for finding the cheapest fuel prices nearby

✓□ Shows real-time updates on gas stations

✓□ Works nationwide

2□□ Eni Station+

✓□ Focuses on Eni fuel stations (one of Italy's biggest chains)

✓□ Includes payment options and discount offers

✓□ Helps find fuel stations with rest areas

3□□ ChargeMap (For Electric Vehicles)

✓□ Best for locating EV charging stations

✓□ Covers Tesla Superchargers and third-party chargers

✓☐ Shows charging speeds and availability in real time

💡 Pro Tip: Fuel stations on highways (Autostrade) are more expensive. Save money by filling up in towns before hitting the motorway.

Final Road Trip Checklist

✅ Navigation Apps Downloaded (Google Maps, Waze, or TomTom)

✅ Parking App Installed (EasyPark or MyCicero)

✅ Fuel App Installed (Prezzi Benzina or Eni Station+)

✅ Emergency Numbers Saved in your phone

✅ Roadside Assistance Plan Ready (Rental car or ACI membership)

✅ Offline Maps Downloaded for rural areas

✅ Toll Payment Plan Prepared (Telepass, Viacard, or cash)

✅ ZTL Zone Awareness (Check maps to avoid fines)

Packing Checklist, Road Etiquette, and Safety Tips for Travelers in Italy

A well-prepared traveler is a stress-free traveler. Whether you're exploring Italy's coastal highways, charming countryside, or bustling cities, having the right essentials will enhance your road trip experience.

In this section, we'll cover:

✓☐ The ultimate packing checklist for road travelers.

✓☐ Essential road etiquette and driving customs in Italy.

✓☐ Safety tips to prevent theft, avoid scams, and handle traffic stops like a pro.

🧳 Packing Checklist for an Italian Road Trip

Packing smart is key to a hassle-free journey. Since you'll be spending a lot of time on the road, it's important to have everything you need to stay safe, comfortable, and entertained.

🚗 Must-Have Car Essentials

✅ Driver's License & International Driving Permit (IDP) – Required for non-EU travelers.

✅ Car Rental Agreement & Insurance Documents – Keep a printed and digital copy.

✅ Roadside Assistance Contact Information – ACI (803 116) or rental company support.

✅ Toll Payment Devices or Cards – Telepass, Viacard, or extra cash for toll booths.

✅ **GPS & Smartphone with Navigation Apps** – Download Google Maps or Waze offline.

✅ **Dash Cam** – Helpful for insurance claims in case of an accident.

✅ **First Aid Kit** – Required by law in Italy.

💡 **Pro Tip:** If renting a car, confirm that it includes mandatory items like a reflective vest, warning triangle, and spare tire—these are legally required in Italy!

👜 **Personal Travel Essentials**

✅ **Valid Passport & Copies** – Keep a digital copy as well.

✅ **Credit/Debit Cards & Cash in Euros (€)** – Some small towns don't accept cards.

✅ **Power Bank & Phone Charger** – Essential for navigation and emergencies.

✅ **Sunglasses & Sunscreen** – Driving in the Italian sun can be intense.

✅ **Comfortable Clothes & Shoes** – Weather varies by region, so pack accordingly.

✅ **Reusable Water Bottle** – Many Italian towns have free, drinkable water fountains.

✅ **Snacks & Non-Perishable Food** – Keep hunger at bay on long drives.

✅ Small Travel Pillow & Blanket – Great for road trip naps.

✅ Notebook & Pen – Handy for jotting down addresses, toll costs, or trip notes.

💡 Pro Tip: If you plan to visit churches or religious sites, carry a light scarf or shawl—some require modest attire for entry.

📱💻 Tech & Entertainment

✅ Spotify or Apple Music Playlists – Download music for when there's no signal.

✅ Audiobooks or Podcasts – Great for long drives.

✅ Camera or GoPro – Capture Italy's breathtaking scenery.

✅ SIM Card or Pocket Wi-Fi – Stay connected without roaming charges.

💡 Pro Tip: Some rental cars don't have USB or Bluetooth connectivity—pack an aux cord just in case!

🇮🇹 Understanding Italian Road Etiquette and Customs

Italian drivers have a reputation for being fast and aggressive, but once you understand the local road culture, driving in Italy becomes much easier.

☐ Key Driving Customs in Italy

✅ Roundabouts Are Common – Always yield to traffic already inside the roundabout.

✅ Left Lane Is for Overtaking – On highways, stay in the right lane unless passing.

✅ Flashing Headlights? Move Over! – If a car behind you flashes its headlights, it's asking you to move aside.

✅ Hand Gestures Are Normal – Italians use hand gestures even while driving! 😄

✅ Traffic Lights Can Be Ignored (by Locals! ☐) – Some drivers in small towns run red lights at night if no one is around. Don't follow their lead!

✅ City ZTL Zones = NO Entry – Many cities have restricted traffic zones (ZTLs) where only locals can drive. Driving into one without permission = big fines!

💡 Pro Tip: Check your rental agreement—some cars have ZTL permits, which allow you to enter restricted areas without fines.

☐ Road Trip Safety: Theft Prevention, Avoiding Scams, and Traffic Stops

While Italy is generally safe, car thefts and scams can happen, especially in tourist-heavy areas. Here's how to keep your possessions and yourself safe.

☐ Preventing Car Theft & Break-Ins

🔒 Always lock your car and close windows when parked.

🎒 Keep valuables hidden – Don't leave bags, cameras, or electronics in sight.

🅿☐ Use secure parking lots – Avoid isolated roadside stops at night.

☐ Beware of "fake mechanics" – Scammers may offer to "fix" your car, only to demand payment afterward.

💡 Pro Tip: If you must leave items in the car, store them in the trunk before arriving at your destination—this prevents thieves from seeing what you left behind.

▬ Avoiding Common Travel Scams in Italy

Unfortunately, Italy has its share of tourist scams. The most typical ones are listed here, along with tips for avoiding them:

1☐ ☐ The "Flat Tire" Scam

🚨 A stranger points out that your tire is flat, offering help. While you're distracted, an accomplice steals from your car.

● How to avoid it? Never accept help from strangers—drive to a gas station instead.

2☐☐ The "Friendly Helper" at ATMs

🚨 Someone offers to "help" you use the ATM but steals your card or PIN.

● How to avoid it? Never accept help while withdrawing money.

3☐☐ The "Accidental Spill" Scam

🚨 A person spills something on you (coffee, ketchup, bird poop) and offers to "help clean up"—while pickpocketing you.

● How to avoid it? Walk away immediately if someone tries to "help" you.

☐ Dealing with Traffic Stops in Italy

If you're pulled over by police in Italy, stay calm and polite. Most traffic stops are routine checks.

👮 Who can stop you?

✓☐ Carabinieri (National Military Police)

✓☐ Polizia Stradale (Highway Patrol)

✓☐ Local Municipal Police

📄 What do they ask for?

✅ Driver's License (IDP if required)

✅ Car Registration & Insurance

✅ Passport (if you're a foreigner)

💡 Pro Tip: If fined, you can often pay on the spot at a discount. Some officers may request cash payments—ask for a receipt to avoid fraud.

ITALY

CHAPTER EIGHT

Interactive Maps and Itineraries for the Ultimate Italian Road Trip

A successful road trip in Italy is all about smart planning and navigation. Whether you're cruising along the Amalfi Coast, exploring Tuscany's rolling hills, or driving through the Dolomites, having detailed maps and pre-planned itineraries ensures a smooth and enjoyable journey.

In this chapter, we'll provide:

📍 **Detailed maps for each major route.**

☐ Suggested itineraries for different trip lengths (3-day, 7-day, and 14-day road trips).

🚗 Essential route highlights to help you plan the perfect Italian adventure.

☐ Detailed Maps for Each Major Route

Northern Italy Road Trips

📌 The Italian Alps & Dolomites Scenic Route – A breathtaking mountain drive through Cortina d'Ampezzo, Val Gardena, and Tre Cime di Lavaredo.

📌 The Lakes Region Road Trip – A picturesque journey around Lake Como, Lake Garda, and Lake Maggiore.

📌 Milan to Venice Cultural Drive – A historic route passing through Verona, Bergamo, and Padua, with wine detours in Franciacorta and Prosecco Wine Road.

Central Italy Road Trips

📌 Tuscany & Chianti Wine Route – Rolling vineyards, historic cities like Florence and Siena, and charming towns like Montepulciano and San Gimignano.

📌 Rome to Florence Historic Highway – A journey through Orvieto, Assisi, and Arezzo, packed with Etruscan history and scenic landscapes.

📌 Umbria & Marche Countryside Drive – Medieval towns, the Adriatic coast, and authentic Italian cuisine.

Southern Italy & Sicily Road Trips

📌 Amalfi Coast & Naples Drive – The iconic coastal route through Positano, Ravello, Sorrento, and Pompeii.

📌 Puglia & Matera Heritage Route – Explore Bari, Alberobello's Trulli houses, and Matera's ancient caves.

📌 Sicily's Grand Tour – A full island loop covering Palermo, Catania, Mount Etna, and the Aeolian Islands.

💡 Pro Tip: Use apps like Google Maps, Waze, or ViaMichelin to get real-time traffic updates and alternative routes.

🚗 Suggested Itineraries: 3-Day, 7-Day, and 14-Day Road Trips

☐ 3-Day Road Trip: A Quick Italian Getaway

Ideal for travelers who want a short but immersive road trip experience.

Option 1: Amalfi Coast Adventure

📅 Day 1 – Start in Naples, visit Pompeii, then drive to Sorrento.

📅 Day 2 – Explore Positano, Amalfi, and Ravello.

📅 Day 3 – Visit Capri (via ferry from Sorrento) or relax in Vesuvius National Park.

Option 2: Tuscany & Chianti Wine Escape

📅 Day 1 – Start in Florence, explore the Uffizi Gallery & Ponte Vecchio.

📅 Day 2 – Drive to Chianti, visit vineyards and Siena.

📅 Day 3 – Discover Montepulciano and San Gimignano, then return to Florence.

💡 Perfect for: Travelers who want a quick but scenic Italian experience.

☐ 7-Day Road Trip: A Classic Italian Journey

This itinerary covers multiple regions while maintaining a relaxed pace.

Option 1: Northern Italy's Best

🗓 Day 1-2 – Explore Milan, drive to Lake Como.

🗓 Day 3 – Visit Lake Garda & Verona.

🗓 Day 4-5 – Explore the Dolomites (Cortina d'Ampezzo, Tre Cime di Lavaredo, Val Gardena).

🗓 Day 6 – Drive to Venice, explore its canals.

🗓 Day 7 – Return to Milan or extend to Bologna.

Option 2: Central Italy's Cultural & Scenic Route

🗓 Day 1-2 – Explore Rome's historic sites.

🗓 Day 3 – Drive to Orvieto and Assisi.

🗓 Day 4-5 – Discover Florence & Chianti wine country.

🗓 Day 6 – Visit San Gimignano and Siena.

🗓 Day 7 – Drive to Pisa & Lucca, then return to Rome.

💡 Perfect for: Travelers who want a blend of culture, nature, and history.

☐ 14-Day Road Trip: The Ultimate Italian Adventure

For travelers who want to fully experience Italy by car.

🗓 Day 1-2 – Rome – Vatican, Colosseum, Trevi Fountain.

📅 **Day 3-4** – Florence & Tuscany – Visit Siena, Chianti, and Montepulciano.

📅 **Day 5-6** – Venice & Verona – Explore the floating city & Juliet's Balcony.

📅 **Day 7-8** – Dolomites & Italian Alps – Drive through Cortina d'Ampezzo & Val Gardena.

📅 **Day 9-10** – Milan & Lake Como – Shop in Milan & relax by the lakes.

📅 **Day 11-12** – Amalfi Coast & Naples – Positano, Ravello, Sorrento.

📅 **Day 13** – Matera & Puglia – Explore cave dwellings & Trulli houses.

📅 **Day 14** – Return to Rome or extend to Sicily.

💡 **Perfect for:** Travelers who want to see Italy's best landscapes, history, and culture.

□ **Customizing Your Itinerary**

♦ Want more nature? Add stops in the Dolomites, Sicily, or the Italian Alps.

♦ Foodie-focused trip? Spend extra time in Bologna, Naples, or Emilia-Romagna.

♦ Love history? Explore Rome, Pompeii, Matera, and Florence in depth.

🔹 Prefer the coast? Focus on Amalfi, Puglia, and the Ligurian Riviera.

💡 Pro Tip: Always check road closures, weather conditions, and holiday schedules when planning your trip!

Alternative Scenic Routes & Digital Resources for a Smooth Italian Road Trip

Italy is famous for its breathtaking landscapes and iconic tourist routes, but during peak seasons, these roads can become crowded and slow-moving. If you prefer a more relaxed journey away from the tourist rush, alternative scenic routes offer a peaceful, authentic experience while still showcasing the country's natural beauty and cultural heritage.

This section provides:

📍 Alternative scenic routes to avoid congested tourist areas.

□ Lesser-known but stunning drives for a more immersive experience.

📲 QR codes for downloadable maps and real-time road updates to help you stay on track.

🚗 Alternative Scenic Routes for Avoiding Crowded Tourist Spots

While Italy's famous routes, like the Amalfi Coast Drive or the Tuscany Wine Road, are spectacular, they also attract millions of tourists every year. If you want to experience Italy's beauty without the crowds, consider these alternative scenic routes.

1. Instead of the Amalfi Coast Drive → Take the Cilento Coast Route

☐ Route: Naples → Paestum → Castellabate → Acciaroli → Marina di Camerota

✅ Why? The Amalfi Coast is stunning but congested. The Cilento Coast (just south of Amalfi) offers similar coastal beauty but with fewer tourists.

✅ Highlights: Ancient Greek ruins in Paestum, quiet fishing villages, and the beautiful Palinuro sea caves.

2. Instead of the Tuscany Wine Route → Try the Maremma Wine Road

☐ Route: Grosseto → Scansano → Pitigliano → Saturnia

✅ Why? The Chianti region is famous but can be overcrowded with wine tourists. Maremma offers rolling vineyards, medieval towns, and thermal baths.

✅ Highlights: Super Tuscan wines, Saturnia's hot springs, and the "tuff cities" of Pitigliano and Sovana.

3. Instead of the Milan-Venice Highway → Take the Po River Delta Drive

☐ Route: Ferrara → Comacchio → Chioggia → Venice

✓ Why? The A4 highway from Milan to Venice is packed with traffic. Instead, explore the Po River Delta, an area of canals, wetlands, and charming fishing towns.

✓ Highlights: Comacchio's "Little Venice", Chioggia's seafood markets, and Ferrara's medieval charm.

4. Instead of the Rome-Florence Highway → Take the Via Cassia

☐ Route: Rome → Viterbo → Bagno Vignoni → Siena → Florence

✓ Why? The main A1 highway is efficient but uninspiring. Instead, the historic Via Cassia follows an ancient Roman road through beautiful Tuscan countryside.

✓ Highlights: Hot springs in Bagno Vignoni, medieval Viterbo, and stunning Siena.

5. Instead of the Dolomites Tourist Route → Try the Friuli-Venezia Giulia Alps Drive

☐ Route: Udine → Cividale del Friuli → Sella Nevea → Tarvisio

✅ Why? The Dolomites are breathtaking but heavily touristed. The Friuli Alps offer similar landscapes with quieter roads and authentic alpine culture.

✅ Highlights: Sella Nevea ski area, border towns with Austrian influences, and Tarvisio's pristine nature trails.

📲 QR Codes for Downloadable Maps & Real-Time Road Updates

To make your trip even smoother, we've included QR codes to access:

📍 Offline maps for each region (Google Maps, Maps.me, or ViaMichelin).

🚧 Live traffic updates and road closures via ANAS (Italy's national road agency).

⛽ Fuel station locations and EV charging points.

🅿 Parking areas and best parking apps.

🚀 **How to Use the QR Codes**

Scan the QR code with your phone camera.

Download the relevant map for offline use.

Use real-time navigation apps for traffic, weather, and road closures.

Sample QR Codes (for illustration only):

📌 Italy Road Conditions (ANAS Live Updates)

🔗 (QR Code here)

📌 Offline Maps for Tuscany Wine Route

🔗 (QR Code here)

📌 Best Parking Apps for Italian Cities

🔗 (QR Code here)

📌 Italy's EV Charging Station Locator

🔗 (QR Code here)

ITALY

CONCLUSION

Final Tips for an Unforgettable Italian Road Trip Experience

As you prepare to embark on your Italian road trip, keeping a few insider tips in mind can make your journey smoother, safer, and even more enjoyable. Here are some final recommendations to ensure that your experience is stress-free, memorable, and filled with adventure.

🚗 **1. Drive Like a Local (But Stay Cautious!)**

Italy's roads are as diverse as its landscapes, and Italian drivers are known for their confident, sometimes aggressive driving style. Here's how to blend in while staying safe:

✓ Roundabouts & Right of Way: Yield to traffic inside the roundabout, and always check for scooters!

✓ City Driving: Be prepared for tight turns, narrow alleys, and aggressive honking—especially in cities like Naples and Rome.

✓ Lane Discipline: On highways, the left lane is strictly for passing. If you linger, expect a flash of headlights behind you!

✓ Scooters & Motorbikes: They will weave through traffic, even on highways. Stay aware and give them space.

☐☐ 2. Always Have an Offline Map

Italy has mountainous regions and rural areas with weak mobile signals. Download offline maps from:

✓ Google Maps (Set routes offline)

✓ Maps.me (Detailed hiking and local roads)

✓ Waze (Great for real-time traffic updates)

Pro Tip: Carry a physical road atlas as a backup in case your phone battery dies or GPS fails!

🅿☐ 3. Master the Art of Parking in Italy

Parking can be tricky and expensive in cities, but knowing the rules helps:

✓ White Lines = Free Parking (but often limited-time zones).

✓ Blue Lines = Paid Parking (use machines or mobile apps like EasyPark).

✓ Yellow Lines = Reserved Parking (for disabled, residents, or taxis).

✓ ZTL Zones (Limited Traffic Areas): If you see a red circle with "ZTL," avoid entering unless you have a permit—or risk a hefty fine!

Pro Tip: Use park-and-ride lots outside major cities to save time and avoid traffic.

⛽ 4. Fueling Up – Know Your Options

✓ Gasoline (Benzina) and Diesel (Gasolio): Be sure to select the correct fuel type!

✓ Self-Serve vs. Full-Service: In rural areas, some stations are self-service only, requiring cash or a card at the pump.

✓ Electric Charging Stations: Italy has an increasing number of EV charging points. Apps like Plenitude+BeeCharge or NextCharge help find them.

Pro Tip: Fuel is more expensive on highways, so fill up in local towns when possible.

🍝 5. Embrace the Local Food Scene

✓ Autogrill Stops: These roadside restaurants are surprisingly good—try fresh paninis, espresso, or local pasta dishes.

✓ Regional Specialties: Each area of Italy has unique food—don't miss out! (Tuscany = Ribollita, Naples = Pizza, Sicily = Arancini).

✓ Siesta Time: Many small-town restaurants close between 2-7 PM, so plan your meals accordingly.

Pro Tip: Ask locals where they eat—the best trattorias are rarely listed online!

☐ 6. Take the Scenic Route & Be Spontaneous

✓ Avoid rushing—some of the best experiences come from unplanned detours.

✓ Look for signs for "Borgo più bello d'Italia"—this marks some of Italy's most beautiful small villages!

✓ Stop for photo opportunities—whether it's a cliffside view, a medieval town, or a vineyard bathed in golden light.

Pro Tip: Drive early in the morning or late in the afternoon to avoid peak traffic and experience Italy's golden hour beauty.

☐ 7. Know What to Do in Case of Emergency

✓ Emergency Numbers:

112 – General Emergency

113 – Police

118 – Medical Assistance

✓ Breakdowns: If your car breaks down, turn on hazard lights, wear a reflective vest, and place a warning triangle behind your car.

✓ Roadside Assistance: Rental companies often provide 24/7 emergency services—save their number!

🎉 Your Italian Road Trip Awaits – Go Make Unforgettable Memories!

By following these final tips, you'll not only avoid common road trip pitfalls but also make the most of Italy's incredible landscapes, rich history, and vibrant culture.

So rev up your engine, roll down the windows, and let the Italian roads lead you to an adventure of a lifetime!

🚗 **Buon viaggio e buon divertimento!**